GYPSY LIVING

Unleash Your Gypsy Spirit
Learn how to live your most daring adventure
each and every day for the rest of your life!

Andrea B. Riggs

BALBOA.
PRESS

A DIVISION OF HAY HOUSE

Balboa Press books may be ordered through booksellers or by contacting:

Balboa Press
A Division of Hay House
1663 Liberty Drive
Bloomington, IN 47403
www.balboapress.com
1 (877) 407-4847

Because of the dynamic nature of the Internet, any web addresses or links contained in this book may have changed since publication and may no longer be valid. The views expressed in this work are solely those of the author and do not necessarily reflect the views of the publisher, and the publisher hereby disclaims any responsibility for them.

The author of this book does not dispense medical advice or prescribe the use of any technique as a form of treatment for physical, emotional, or medical problems without the advice of a physician, either directly or indirectly. The intent of the author is only to offer information of a general nature to help you in your quest for emotional and spiritual well-being. In the event you use any of the information in this book for yourself, which is your constitutional right, the author and the publisher assume no responsibility for your actions.

Any people depicted in stock imagery provided by Thinkstock are models, and such images are being used for illustrative purposes only. Certain stock imagery © Thinkstock.

Print information available on the last page.

ISBN: 978-1-5043-8100-0 (sc)
ISBN: 978-1-5043-8099-7 (hc)
ISBN: 978-1-5043-8101-7 (e)

Library of Congress Control Number: 2017908376

Balboa Press rev. date: 11/15/2017

dedication

To all of the gypsies across the globe who identify with me and *Gypsy Living*- welcome home.

Contents

foreword

By Baron Baptiste

It always amazes me what is accomplished when people are committed to pause, put their life on a shelf and really look and listen to what their bigger purpose is. Andrea did just that, and Gypsy Living is an example of what can be accomplished when you are both aligned and committed to your message. Her journey began on her mat with Baptiste Yoga and her consistent practice is what has taken her to accomplish this body of work. I encourage you to take your time with this book and enjoy each moment. May we all find the personal journey that seeks us and leads us to living life fully and powerfully.

—BARON BAPTISTE

preface

"Twenty years from now you will be more disappointed by the things you didn't do than by the ones you did do. So throw off the bowlines. Sail away from the safe harbor. Catch the trade winds in your sails. Explore. Dream. Discover".

—MARK TWAIN

You have done it! You have "thrown off the bowlines" and are ready to unleash you and your family's gypsy spirit and live an adventurous life! You have taken the first step towards creating the life of your dreams and that begins with the one person you have control over—YOU!

Now take a deep breath, hold it, and slowly exhale.

Did you do it?

That was your first test. I know it seems simple and it is, yet how often do we listen to advice that others offer us, but do nothing with this gift. This is what I call *a failure to put it into practice*. If you did not do it the first time, this is your second chance. Remember…life is always filled with second chances, so begin embracing them now.

Take a deep breath and hold it...*Count 1, 2, 3, 4, 5.* Now slowly exhale.

Why is being aware of our breathing so important?

Breath is life. It is the ebb and flow of bringing in and letting go. Without it, one cannot survive yet many people take shallow, short breaths, which can be a reflection of living shallow lives. It can also be a signal of an inability to take in life fully. In each of my fitness classes, I bring awareness to breathing through the difficult movements because too often, we stop breathing through the difficult or challenging aspects of our lives. In time you will be a pro (if you are not one already) at simply breathing through life. Through this simple breath, you will learn the art of flowing through, and eventually even dancing through life.

I believe we all have a gypsy spirit, filled with desire, passion, life, vibrancy, energy, confidence, and flow. Your gypsy spirit is the embodiment of your essence and what makes you, YOU. Most women do not realize how amazing they are. Feelings of inferiority, doubt, unworthiness, and an overwhelming sense of "just not good enough" tend to cloud their energy, judgement, and ultimately blind them to their real potential.

The lesson is that *you* are bright and colorful! You are a dreamer, a wanderer, and a human who holds her head high. One who has many tricks up her sleeve and probably lots of ointments, Band-Aids, and anything else you carry with you. You *are* prepared with everything needed right at this moment.

You will never attain the greatness life has in store for you until you are consistently living in a state of gypsy love for yourself, your family, and all you are doing. Realize that you are solely in control of your own life. The time has come to embrace this knowledge, breathe deep, and spread your arms up to the heavens, accepting the power and ability you have to change yourself. By doing so, you will begin to do more for the human race than you ever dreamed possible.

I have a great sense of gratitude for you and those who have been with me on my journey of life. Join me now in feeling gratitude for the mothers and fathers, angels, and all positive forces in our lives who have influenced and been there for us. Life gives us what we believe it will. People will show up for us when we need them, believe this to be true and know that you will never walk alone again.

introduction

why i wrote this book

Having successfully created my dream life, filled with exploration and adventure with my husband and children, my mission has become to help others embrace their unique selves by realizing their invaluable worth. Through my books, I aim to encourage my community to tap into their creative gypsy spirits to learn how much abundace is out there for them. As they learn to cultivate the positive energy that lies within them, they create space to receive more emotional, physical, financial, and spiritual abundance.

By the time I was married, I was a world traveler and one could argue that I was already tainted by the gypsy ways – an early foreboding of wonderlust. At a young age, I realized how precious life is and how much there is to see, experience, and partake of in this world. It was within these moments of reflection and gratitude that my gypsy spirit was born.

When I met the love of my life, I realized that he had not travelled the world as much as I had even though he had a desire to do so. He also had a hunger and an unquenchable thirst to explore, seek truth, live, and to surpass any self-imposed limits. Together we've hitched our caravans—living, working, and exploring with our three little gypies, who are our greatest inspiration and treasures. Adventure has always been the air we've breathed. For my husband and I, immersing ourselves in nature—whether we are being still, playing, seeking or exploring—is not a novelity, but a necessity. It runs in our blood and is something we crave above all else.

Although becoming a gypsy can be simple for some, I've begun to undersand why there are so many (women especially) who are hiding their inner beauty and power—which I call their gypsy spirits. I began to recognize the sharp contrast between living an adventurous life and living a life struggling between hiding who you are and finding your identity.

Throughout my journey I have discovered specific tools that I used to uncover my own inner gypsy spirit. That wisdom is held within the contents and energy of this book. I'm compelled to share it because I believe that one person's journey can massivly change the course of another's life. There have been many books that have done this for me. As I open my gypsy heart and allow my meaningful life lessons to flutter around you like butterflies, my intention is that your life will change for the better, forever.

I wrote this book to unite the women who run the world by offering them the beauty of living an adventurous gypsy life. I wrote this book my friend, for you, for me, and for our future generations. For when we lift up one, we lift up many. The world is a better place when we join hands as energy beings, who love ourselves and who love to dance, express, and explore.

introduction

why should you read this?

Gypsy Living will help you embrace your gypsy spirit by providing you with tools to create the life you want. I believe by utilizing the contents within this book, you CAN and WILL live your most daring adventure! This information can teach you how to live more spontaneously. *How?* By helping you to see life as an adventure, through a unique perspective that offers avenues that are much more exciting than you ever thought possible.

Within you lies *your* gypsy spirit, which is inherently glorious by design. Sadly, due to limiting beliefs about what you believe *is* possible for you, you have learned to survive instead of thrive. Your life is meant to be filled with abundance, exploration, and adventure! You are meant to experience the glee of capturing your dreams, the surprise of the ocean waves in your face, and the stillness of the night stars in the desert. You are meant to sink your teeth into life and drink of the blissful nectar that fills your soul with energy, peace, and connection. Your life is your creation, what will you create? The world is waiting for your gypsy spirit to become unleashed so you can bless your own life and the lives of those you love. Only when you embrace your tremendous worth will you learn to harness the attributes of a G.Y.P.S.Y. and live your most daring adventure.

Do you have untapped potential or any internal disaccord? It may be your gypsy spirit fighting to get out! Embracing your inner gypsy takes a gentle process of self-discovery. We will do this together through awareness and acknowledgement by learning the art of embracing, recognizing, and letting go with the varied tools I have learned along my gypsy path.

By connecting with our inner gypsy at the deepest level, we awaken the fire inside that allows us to reconnect to ourselves. When we open our new gypsy eyes, we begin to see life's adventures that were not there before.

By the end of our journey, you will master the art of unleashing your own gypsy spirit so you and your family can live a more adventurous life. The information I offer will help you get in touch with your deepest gypsy desires, intuition, and spirit. Don't worry—there is no fluff, fillers, expectations, judgement, or competition. All that I ask is for you to ride this wave on your own. This is a safe and sacred journey—one all about you.

Why should you read this book? Because you are worth it. You are worthy of all the love, success, abundance, peace, and joy this life has to give. Life has so much to offer you, if you will but open your eyes, heart, and soul. Are you ready to join me on a great adventure? Are you ready to tap into your larger purpose? Are you ready to do the work that will change the way you live, for the rest of your life? I hope so!

workbook

A word about this book and the word that encompasses a possibly negative connotation for some—work.

Don't misunderstand, everything in life is work. Every decision and action takes work. Think about it…each time you zip up your jeans and take out the trash, you are doing the work. Personally, I love to work on my mat during my yoga practice and I love to work in the kitchen making delicious food for my family (most of the time). I assure you that work can feel good and I would love for you to do this work for yourself.

With so much work going on, you would think we as humans would think to do the work on our insides as well. Typically, we don't. I get it; it can be scary to look inside. Some of you will think you have this in the bag, let me assure you, we all have work to do on a consistent and ongoing basis. Wherever you are at in your life, know that I honor your journey, as you in turn honor mine.

I have designed this book as a workbook so that you are able to write your thoughts and feelings, while doing the work along with me. Remember, it is meant to challenge your entire belief system. If you are not willing to do the work and be honest with yourself, that is okay. There will come a time, a day, or a moment when you are able to breathe, let go, and be honest with yourself.

If you would like to read or listen to this book one or one hundred times without lifting a finger, be my guest. Only you know when you are ready to begin *doing* the work. You are the only one who can determine if your answers are coming from your head or your heart. It's up to you to do the work that will change the way you live, for the rest of your life.

You will also see doodle pages at the end of each chapter. These are for you to do whatever your heart desires. You may sketch or draw images, circles, flowers, fish, hearts, or anything! You can write, express, and allow your gypsy spirit to become unleashed through your pen and paper.

With that my friend, know that I love you. I did not write this book by chance. I have tested the limits of my knowledge, expanded past what has been possible for me, sunk my teeth into the marrow of life, and done the work. When you are ready to do the work, I will be right here, and your workbook will be open and non-judgmental, ready to show you just how magnificent you and your gypsy spirit truly are.

The Promise of *Gypsy Living:*

I promise that as you read and work through *Gypsy Living*, you will come alive.

> *"Don't ask what the world needs. Ask what makes you come alive, and go do it. Because what the world needs is people who have come alive."*

— HOWARD THURMAN

I

creation of a gypsy

"Every act of creation is first an act of destruction."

—PABLO PICASSO

You are the creator of your life. It is in your very nature and DNA to persevere and thrive. While most people spend their lives merely surviving, a gypsy thrives. There is a broad distinction between these two. Surviving throughout one's life is a reactive behavioral trait—the "victim" mentality. It is the belief that life happens to you and you have no control over it. We are aiming to go above and beyond thriving to unleash, flourish, and learn to live as a true creator.

I believe that regardless of your struggle, you can overcome, heal, and move forward by utilizing certain tools. There is a reason for your journey and while you may have internal struggles, it is those very challenges that offer you the ability to have empathy for others.

What if I told you that you create your life and that you have the most powerful weapon on Earth already inside of you? Would you believe me? I invite you to believe this statement, even if it is difficult. I ask you to open your mind and ask yourself these two simple questions: *Do I create my life? Is the life I am living exactly what I would choose or are there areas I would like to change?*

Of course, we will be focusing on how to improve your gypsy spirit! This is your spirit of extraordinary adventure, full of more excitement than you can imagine. I promise you that the tools in this book will assist you in doing just that. I believe in your ability to create the life you want. Being the creator of your life means that you are in the driver's seat and you take 100% responsibility for your ability to fulfill your own dreams.

You may say, "How can I think about living out my adventure if my family or life is falling apart?"

Divorce, bankruptcy, health crises, mental illness, and addiction, you name it, they are increasing massively. In *Secrets of the Millionaire Mindset,* the author claims that 80% of people are unhappy, unfulfilled, and not as financially successful as they wanted to be by the time they die. I aim to change that, with women specifically. Throughout this book, you will be faced with many decisions. You can choose to change or you can choose to stay the same. The choice is yours. Consider this a wake-up call, from yourself.

I have lived long enough to know that nothing in the following pages is necessarily right, wrong, true, or false. It is simply my experience. You are welcomed to throw out what does not work for you and take what does. I will leave that up to you and your own intuition. Complete this workbook in its entirety, doing all of the work, and let the information and exercises seep into your soul. Sooner than you think, the pull of your gypsy spirit will begin to rise up and you will realize all that life has in store for you. The energy of the life you have always dreamed of is waiting for you.

Let's get started...

When it comes to self-reflection, it is very possible that you are judgmental, critical, and even self-abusive. Self-criticisms and self-sabotage have been a cause of the gypsy spirit's destruction since the beginning of time. Let's take a moment to make this a little more intimate for us. Imagine I am calling you over the phone and asking you a very direct question, *"Are you happy?"*

Stop and really think about this question, and after you have thought about it, feel it.

How does your heart feel? _____
_____
_____

What would the outcome of that phone call be?_____
_____
_____

How would you respond?_____
_____
_____

What would you think?_____
_____
_____

It is important to determine the amount of priority you give your own happiness. What amount of attention are you willing to offer yourself to actualize self-fulfillment?

Do you typically trade your happiness for another's happiness—specifically the happiness of your spouse or loved ones?_____

You may have noticed my foreword is written by author, yoga teacher and Baptiste Institute Creator, Baron Baptiste. He is one of my mentors and he has greatly impacted my life. At his trainings, he continually asks participants to *consider.* What does Baron mean by *considering?* Repeatedly he will say, "Just consider this is true and be curious." He's asking his students to consider that they're hiding behind a mask and not staying true to themselves. Being open to pondering that we are in fact hiding something, is the only path to staying true to yourself. Consider we have disempowering beliefs and that we make decisions to a certain extent, based on those beliefs. Is there a better way? Yes. Living in your true north and being in your power is how you begin unleashing your gypsy spirit. It is the opposite of hiding.

As you breathe the breath of life, you will redefine the meaning of life. As you push the envelope and the boundaries of mediocrity, you will break out of limited cultural ways of thinking—shattering your entire paradigm of beliefs. I embrace you now as you wake up and take responsibility for your life, and for the lives of the humans you may be raising. You *are* the change.

Action Exercise:

> You and I are sitting on comfy cushions in the middle of a forest where it is the perfect temperature for you. Nearby a waterfall cascades into a pond covered with lily pads, purple flowers, and green leaves. Butterflies

and fireflies flutter through the lush and fragrant air as dusk sets in.

Are you there? Can you see it and smell it?

Stop reading, close your eyes, and visualize this. If you are listening, then do this now with me. Really, do it. We are comfortable. There is nothing to do, nowhere to go. No kids to pick up or drop off. No groceries melting in the car. No dinner to prepare. No emails to send off, no work meetings or conference calls to attend, and no family drama. This is your time to be present.

Take a deep breath.

Don't worry about doing it the right way or perfectly, just breathe deep, filling your lungs completely, and then slowly exhale.

You and I are together in our first meditation, mindfulness, or chilling out session. We are sitting and allowing ourselves to use one another's eyes as a mirror. While this is uncomfortable for many to do in real life, this exercise is a powerful tool that will open the gateway between us which will allow my words to penetrate your gypsy spirit, alleviate the pain, and help her shine through you.

Now, breathe with me. Inhale: 1, 2, 3, 4. Hold 2, 3 4, and exhale 1,2,3,4.

Again. Repeat 5 times.

Remember that the more you exhale, the larger your inhale must be. Concentrate on expelling the old air from your lungs completely.

Good work, keep going. Not only are you accomplishing the action exercise, but you are also learning how to breathe like a gypsy.

See how long you can do this breathing exercise. Try it first for 1 minute and then work up to 5 minutes.

Exercise complete.

Breathing is a fundamental part of your journey of discovery and plays a key role in the development of your gypsy spirit. It helps us answer those difficult questions—who are you, where have you been hiding, and why?

This moment is a chance to change your life and to become more in line with your gypsy spirit—one who wanderlusts and travels with the intention to roam wherever the wind of her intuition may guide her. Learning to live a life in tune with your own gypsy spirit is a process. However, this does not come without its own challenges.

Changing is not as simple as just reading this book. Real change comes from going within, reflecting, and answering difficult questions for yourself. Your gypsy spirit quite possibly has been suppressed for most of your life. Nevertheless, it is there waiting for you to redeem it. The only way to do this is if you are willing to be vulnerable and have absolute trust in the process. Therefore, in order to continue you must trust me, you must trust yourself, and you must trust the Universe.

There is a considerable chance that you are living with a twinge of regret or resentment, and a lack of fulfillment. Maybe you have a burning desire to get out into the world and explore, but you dash those dreams for staying safe, secure, and stable. If you are willing to take action, you will unleash your gypsy spirit and open your life to more success, adventure, love, light, and truth than you have ever dreamed possible!

I learned this next exercise from author and speaker Louise Hay in her book, *You Can Heal Your Life*. I have used it with clients and have found it offers awareness and empowerment.

Action Exercise:

1. Write down all of the problems in your life.

   _____
   _____
   _____

2. Write down all the things you should be doing in your life.

   _____
   _____
   _____

3. Now replace *should* with *could*.

   _____
   _____
   _____

4. Write for 5 minutes about how you feel about the
    energy shift when you changed *should* to *could*.

    _____

    _____

    _____

    _____

    _____

    _____

    _____

    _____

    _____

    _____

    _____

    _____

    _____

    _____

    _____

    _____

    _____

    _____

    _____

    _____

    _____

    _____

    _____

    _____

    _____

    _____

    _____

    _____

5. Write down the real problem in your life. *Hint: the only real problem is connected to the way you view yourself, the unworthiness you feel or not feeling good enough to do what you want in life.*

_____

_____

_____

6. What would you like to create in your life?

_____

_____

_____

7. If you could do anything with your life, what would it be?

_____

_____

_____

8. What is really holding you back from living your life the way you choose?

_____

_____

_____

You have now completed the exercise. If you have not written down your answers, go for it! Get it messy! Scribble and make it your own! No one ever has to see these words except you. I encourage you to do it now before you proceed to the next chapter. I believe in you and know that when you begin to open up to your true feelings about yourself and your life, magic will begin to happen.

DOODLE PAGE

II

freeing your inner gypsy

"Our freedom can be measured by the number of things we can walk away from."

—VERNON HOWARD

Freedom to live the life you choose comes at a cost. You have to learn to let go of a lot. The better you get at letting go, the more your gypsy spirt can become unleashed. Undoubtedly, you will have some inner turmoil throughout this process. This is natural so be gentle with yourself. As you focus on creating the life you want, you will be pulled towards solution-oriented thinking instead of the survival mentality. In other words, the more you focus on creating the "I can's" in your life, the easier it will become to live aligned with your gypsy spirit.

When you choose to let your gypsy spirit guide you through life, you are free. In this chapter, we will seek to bridge the gap and learn how to free your inner gypsy. I will ask you to do more exercises and it's important to remember to be willing to laugh at yourself, giggle inside, and let go of what you think others think about you. Learning to laugh at yourself is an important key to unleashing your inner gypsy.

Action Exercise:

1. First, what are you willing to let go of? What can you easily walk away from in order to free yourself? I.E.— we moved from Arlington, Virginia with just a uBox and I learned that stuff is really just stuff. Or maybe yours will look more like, I am willing to let go of my ego.

    Make a list:

    _____
    _____
    _____
    _____
    _____

2. As you look through this list, I want you to become introspective about each of your answers. If you are willing to walk away from your career, why? If you are having trouble in a relationship, why? What is it you have been holding onto in your life that is causing this resistance?

    _____
    _____
    _____
    _____
    _____

When you resist anything in life, it persists. You've probably heard the saying by Carl Jung, "That which you resist, persists." The more you hate someone or something, and the more irritated you are about a situation, the more it is going to hang around you. How you feel about life and the way you internalize your world matters. Despite the fast-paced life you lead, the fact of the matter is you probably struggle internally.

What is the real problem in our lives? Earlier, I mentioned Louise Hay and her book, *You Can Heal Your Life*. In it, she mentions that all problems come down to one concept—not feeling worthy or good enough. Any problem in your life, at the root cause, boils down to this feeling of hopelessness that you do not measure up. Therefore, in order to unleash your gypsy spirit and be free, you must go within.

I invite you now to go within and move into the deepest valley of your own personal torment and guilt. Uncover and unload the hurt, shame, anguish, and unworthiness that lies hidden there. Be willing to be vulnerable. Take out the dirtiest, darkest memories and feelings and then go back for more. Get it out, and finally clean out the darkest corners of your head and heart.

Take a moment here to breathe, visualize this and imagine I am right there with you for each item, memory, and resentment.

It will feel uncomfortable, but it is possible for you to let go of your dark memories and feelings. Remember, it's imperative that you treat yourself with compassion while letting go of who you are not, to allow more space for the person you are becoming. Embrace your gypsy spirit that has been screaming to get out and to allow your future to unfold in a beautiful and mystical way. Resist nothing.

Visualization Exercise:

Close your eyes. I am going to take you
into a visualization. This will allow you to
prepare for this journey. Take a deep breath
and close your eyes. Imagine you are in a
town square. You are standing in the middle
of the square on a tall mountain of old false
beliefs and paradigms. Now pick up the
sledgehammer next to you and shatter your
foundation. Everything you think you know
about yourself, your family, your culture, your
existence, your religion, your life, and your
happiness…all of it. Break it up, smash it, and
see the dust fly! Have fun, smile and don't
worry! Anything that brings light, love, and
abundance to your life will remain.

You are powerful!

Now, simply see where the dust settles.
What is left? You, standing in the middle
with cement dust all over your body, in your
hair and all over your face. In fact, I can see
right now it may seem pretty "dooms-day-
ish"! You are there, but all I can see is rubble,
dust, and your eyes.

Now, walk out of the rubble. Take a breath.
Another deeper breath. Walk. Keep walking.
Walk and walk, and just keep walking.

The dust is beginning to fall away now and
with the separation of space between you

and your foundation, you are beginning to feel space. Congratulations! You have created this beautiful space.

There is a beautiful, clean, clear jungle (bug and crocodile free) with vines to swing on. Hop on a vine and swing effortlessly into the air. Now go ahead, let go, and float about twenty feet into the crystal clear pond. Imagine hands gently guiding you safely to the pond below. You are weightless.

Feel the wetness of the pure cool water as it welcomes your body. Notice how deep your breath permeates your lungs. Now take another breath and hold it before sinking into the glistening water. Feel your body sink deeper and deeper, and as you go deeper, you can see every particle of your old foundation slip off your soul, your skin, your mind and your heart. Let it float away—all the judgments, expectations, and competition that surrounded you and your life before are gone. Also gone is the old you, along with your old beliefs about what life was supposed to be. Gone is the belief that you don't measure up. Gone are the false needs that were not yours to begin with.

Slowly let the air begin to trickle out of your nostrils. Notice your inherent will to rise up. If you feel good in this place, stay there as long as you need to let all of the black poison seep out your pours. Notice what you are letting go of. It could be darkness in any shape or form.

When you are ready, I want you to see your gypsy spirit begin to glow within you as a magnificent blue light. This is your light and power that has been inside of you all along.

Journal about your feelings.

What is coming up for you? Does this seem silly, freeing, or introspective? Was this exercise hard for you? What do you notice about the inner voices in your head?

_____

_____

_____

_____

_____

_____

_____

_____

_____

_____

_____

_____

_____

_____

_____

_____

_____

_____

_____

In the past, you may have given your power away easily. Whether it was your dreams, hopes, people, business, ideas, potential and opportunities, but not anymore. No longer will you allow anyone to walk all over you or take advantage of you. You are magnificent, worthy of love, kindness, beauty, abundance, money, time and everything else you desire. You will forever be powerful as long as you keep this in mind and always honor your power.

If you are reading, take a moment and fully sit with yourself and this imagery. Visualization will change you if you allow it. How do you feel?

Visualization Exercise Continued:

> When you are ready, begin to feel as if you are naturally allowing your body to float upwards. Notice your feet and the way they flitter against the water in order to propel your body upward towards air, life, and your journey through your greatest adventure.

> As you emerge from the water, listen to your breath as you inhale deeply. Welcome to your gypsy journey. This is your birth into taking control of your power. You are now tapped into your gypsy spirit and are free to explore. Welcome!

How do you feel?

_____

_____

_____

_____

Are you excited and ready for the next exercise? You will have action exercises in each chapter, however, initially to get us started we needed to first cleanse and then root. Now it is time to root.

For the second exercise, we will begin with aligning the chakras. If you aren't familiar with the term, chakras are energy wheels or disks in the body. If you have ever been to an acupuncturist they gently tap needles into your meridians. Here is an analogy, if the chakras are the seven states within (around) our body, then the meridians are the cities within the states. These energy centers and pathways are all connected by streets or what we've heard called circulation.

A good question is...what good is energy flow and circulation if the way many of us are internalizing our world constantly shuts down entire chakras? Deepak Chopra tells us, "Chakras are junction points between consciousness and physiology. These centers of energy govern the core emotional and physical functions of your being. When these energy centers are congested or out of harmony, your vital life force is unable to freely circulate, resulting in distress, disease, and lack of mind-body integrity."

As you gain your own enlightenment on this introspective journey, keep in mind that these tools will help set you free. It won't happen after doing this just once. It is a continuous practice of listening with your heart and feeling your way through.

This image may help you visualize what we just discussed. I encourage you to color in the corresponding colors noted below. Have fun and be creative! Imagine you are 6 years old again while coloring.

For an example see my website:

(photo credit www.theChakras.org.)

Visualization Exercise:

1. Visualize the color red at the first chakra at the base of your spine and think, *I belong in this world and my personal needs are always met. I root and belong wherever I go because I know I am meant to be here at this time. I am worthy of being alive. I belong to a tribe much larger than I ever knew. I am accepted and loved.*

2. Visualize the color orange at the second chakra midway between the base of your spine and your belly

button and think, *I recognize that I am the creator of my life and am worthy of all the good, success, and abundance life has to offer and which I desire.*

3. Visualize the color yellow above your navel and think, *I own and protect my own personal power, which lovingly encompasses me in white and gold light, guiding and protecting me. I allow myself to be protected from others energy who may be stronger than mine, so that I do not take on their negative or aggressive energy.*

4. Visualize the color green in the center of your chest and think, *I love freely and lead with an open heart with the realization that my heart is the center where mind, body, spirit, and emotions all collide together to create the unstoppable gypsy spirit. Once unleased, it will guide, direct, and keep me in tune with the call of the ultimate life force that speaks to me.*

5. Visualize the color light blue at your throat and think, *I speak my gypsy truth, no matter the consequence because my words matter, are powerful, and need to be heard. I speak with love, connection, and a warm embrace to assist others on their journey and bring those searching into the gypsy fold. There is always room and my words are powerful, unique, and hold universal organizing power.*

6. Visualize the color bright blue bleeding into purple in the center of your forehead and think, *my gypsy heart is directly linked to my third eye, my intuition, and encompasses the gypsy spirit as a whole. It is through this wisdom and assurance that I act, allowing the heart to lead and the mind to work out the details. When working together this union creates a full life, lived through the gypsy spirit.*

7. Visualize the color vibrant purple at the top of your head and think, *this symbolizes the perfect union of body, mind, and spirit. The trifecta of spiritual connection to my highest gypsy self, connecting me to others and to a source that is the ultimate force for good in the world. I am a part of something much bigger than myself. I am a vehicle for good, for love, for consciousness and am an integral piece of the web of life. I am known and cared for and I am a creator in every sense of the word.*
Take a deep cleansing breath and notice how relaxed and energetic you feel. We will go deeper into this type of work in the *reflection* chapter.

For a free guided chakra opening with me go to www.GypsyFam.com/GypsyLivingTips

These seven key points assist you in tapping into your true nature. Through this balancing of connection between yourself and others, you will find abundance, love, light, truth, peace, and the freedom to use your talents. This freedom aligns you with your deepest desires. You will soon use your talents with pure intent to create abundance for yourself, your family, and all those close to you.

This exercise has the ability to root you to what is most grounding in your life. It may be relationships to people or to the metaphysical. For me, the unseen is more grounding than anything I can see with my physical eyes. This sense of peace, energy, light, love and prana allows us to become grounded enough that we feel safe to take flight.

I believe that we are all connected to a tremendously positive feminine energy force. It is from this source that both you and I are tethered and will forever be connected. This is how we ground ourselves to this place, which always calls our gypsy spirit back. It is a place full of peace, comfort, and serenity.

Take this knowledge with you as you embark on your journey, and if at any point you begin to feel overwhelmed, frustrated, or at a loss, be still and breathe. Know that this book moves quickly and since it is yours for life, take it as slowly as you need to. Be patient and compassionate with yourself, letting go of what you think the outcome should look like. There is no right way for this journey to unfold. Allow it to be what it is. Resist nothing. Breathe and learn to let go.

Action Exercise:

If this seems silly, look more closely at your life. If what you have been doing is not working, while this may seem a bit crazy, what do you have to lose? At the very least, you can try something new and see what happens! The results may surprise you.

What comes up for you? How do you feel? Do you feel any resistance? Go deeper and discover why...

_____

_____

_____

_____

_____

_____

With this awareness of your gypsy chakras, you are now ready to go even more deeply on your journey into unleashing your gypsy spirit. The foundation of becoming a gypsy stems from 5 key values. We will explore these in the next five chapters.

They are:

1. **(G)ratitude** - for life and the abundance all around you.
2. **(Y)es** - to YOU!
3. **(P)ositive Purpose** - the intent in all you do.
4. **(S)elf-Love** - encompasses the limitless confidence you have within your soul for self-expression.
5. **(Y)oung at heart** - because all gypsies love to play, dance, laugh, and enjoy life...even embracing the times they trip.

DOODLE PAGE

III

"G" is for gratitude

"Gratitude is the healthiest of all human emotions. The more you express gratitude for what you have, the more likely you will have even more to express gratitude for".

—ZIG ZIGLAR

G IS FOR GRATITUDE OF LIFE AND THE ABUNDANCE ALL
AROUND YOU

We are now going to begin working on creating gratitude and thankfulness in each moment of your life. Gratitude stems from the heart. It is genuine and tender, bringing with it a sense of peace, trust, and happiness.

I believe life is meant to be lived from the heart, connecting with others through an open heart and mind. It is quite possible that you have been living your life through your head, allowing logic to direct most of your decisions. The problem with this is that you can think your way into and out of many circumstances in life. You probably analyze, simulate, and are constantly trying to figure it all out. While it may seem like the smart way to live, in actuality it adds to stress and unhappiness, ultimately leading to an ungrateful heart.

I'm not saying don't use your mind. It is there for a reason and it definitely helps take you where you need to go. The key is to let the heart lead, allowing the mind to be the driver for the heart. The heart should be the decision maker, while the brain works out the details.

Learning to get in touch with your heart by living from it allows your world to open up rapidly. You will become grateful for yourself, your choices, and the goodness you have brought into your own life. All gratitude begins within. Once you have mastered (or at least are on the road), you can easily become grateful for more and more aspects of your life. Try it, I guarantee your stress levels will be reduced, you will find clarity, peace, and gain the ability to say "yes" to the things that matter and "no" to the things that do not.

Becoming a thankful person is easy, fun, and freeing. By simply thinking and feeling (feeling is KEY here) thankfulness you can begin to cultivate new neural pathways in your brain and move into a place of openness, awareness, and connectedness to your life. Being grateful on a daily basis helps you to let go of your ego as you begin to realize that you do not have to be anyone other than who you are. This is learned through the process of getting in touch with the aspects of yourself for which you become thankful.

It is possible that gratefulness comes easier to you than others, or vice versa. When you look around do you see abundance, or is your world lacking? Realize in this moment that the lens (your own point of view) may have become foggy and scratched. Take off the lenses and clean them up now.

Visualization Exercise:

For fun, I have written a poem for each of the five gypsy characteristics chapters so they will stick with you more deeply. Along with each precious value, you will find there is also a corresponding "demon" to be on the lookout for.

I invite you now to visualize with me while listening to this story.

I once saw a gypsy hunched over with sunken eyes and black teeth. She had been poisoned by a demon of the night. His name was **Censure.** I walked up to her full of compassion and asked her simply, "What has caused this pain I see deep in your eyes?"

Full of spite and bitterness, she told me about a day far gone when another had come her way. These were her words:

I once was loved by a man so dear,
One who longed for my touch, and
whose intent was clear.
I gave him my heart and my soul unbidden,
little did I know what was in store lay hidden.
Hidden from my heart and mind was my own fear,
a subject that would convince even heaven's tears.
Fears for want of fortune and riches,
the happiness I found in a new man's wishes.
It did not take me long however to see,
how my own censure had corrupted me.

For now, I was in a deep dark hole,
and I had traded true love,
for a life of misery and woe.
My story is sad and I am left with remorse,
for a life I had, that unfortunately I lost.
Would that I had known then, the cost
of my lack of gratitude.
For my own life's goals and missions were skewed,
for the life that was mine, the love of a man,
was all that I needed.
If only sweet gratitude I would have seeded.

This simple poem demonstrates the pain that can be felt when you are unable to see the greatness in your own life by feeling genuine gratitude for people and circumstances. This woman had all she needed, yet buried deep inside was a belief that she needed a man with money to be happy.

Afterwards, she soon realized that riches meant nothing and what she had with the man she loved was more precious than money, fame, or fortune. Her previous belief that it was "just love" blinded her ability to see life's true gifts. Life will always have an opposing force like good versus evil. In this poem, **the demon to watch out for was censure**, which is to express severe disapproval of someone or something.

What beliefs do you have about happiness? What do you believe will bring you happiness?

My hope is for you, my friend, to learn to harness the ability to see the important mysteries of life and always extend gratitude for them before it is too late.

Can you locate your internal switch telling you that you disapprove of something or someone? In the poem, her own severe disapproval (at a deep internal level) was a fear of living a life without money. When you are consumed and constantly focused on what you do *not* have, you lose sight of the epic day-to-day journey. You fail to see that life's greatest mysteries many times turn out to be your biggest blessings and greatest adventures.

Having an attitude of gratitude is all about the small things in life—the tiny details in nature, relationships, in our homes, and in our interactions. Once focused upon, we have the ability to shift our entire way of thinking. Oprah Winfrey said, "Be thankful for what you have; you'll end up having more. If you concentrate on what you don't have, you will never, ever have enough."

While it is natural to have emotional up's and down's and days that you feel more grateful than another, it is possible to always be aware of the act, skills, and movement towards gratitude. This means that while today you may not "feel" a deep sense of joy, you can become aware of it in your mind and set an intention to feel it more deeply. It is through this awareness and intention setting that more space will come in. You may be surprised at how quickly you begin to feel more joy.

Being a grateful person comes easier to some than others. Don't feel discouraged if it is more difficult for you. Just like working out at the gym, it takes time to build muscle.

Similarly, your gratitude muscle needs time, attention, and dedication to become stronger.

Why do some have an easier time with this than others? Because of life experiences which can be internalized differently. If you have resentments or regrets, many times they show up as anger and fear. While harboring these powerfully negative emotions, gratitude can be difficult to muster because you are too busy resisting that event in your life.

Sometimes life and the journey within ourselves can seem long. I guarantee you it will feel even longer and harder if you do not choose to see the good that oozes from every pour of your being. *In Man's Search for Meaning* by Viktor E. Frankl, he tells his story of being held in a concentration camp in Germany in World War II. His wife died in a separate camp and everything he loved was stripped from him. He writes, "Our greatest freedom is the freedom to choose our attitude." His epic account of life, gratitude, and attitude have stuck with me my entire life. I guarantee if we were sitting around a table and we all threw out our problems, you would be extremely quick to gather yours right back up. No one has power over you, only you have the power to change your attitude. You are in control 100% of the time.

You have so much to be grateful for so now is the time to open your eyes, see it, verbalize it, and fully feel it.

There will always be hard days because you are human and you are given the space and freedom to make choices—to fail, succeed, hurt, love, react, and respond. Note that wanting to act out in a negative manner is simply a feeling, an emotion. Just like the wave that rolls onto the shore, it will crash, and then subside. What you choose to give weight and attention to matters. You have the ability when faced with negative self-views, inner turmoil, and negative emotions to breathe, let it go, and not react.

You are meant to flow through life with ease and grace, breathing in goodness and feeling the sunlight on your face. You are meant to trust in the Universe and when you do, the world opens up to you. When you make a conscious choice to embrace the simple act of releasing that which does not serve you, you begin removing the disease of fear.

The road to gratitude is through awareness and acknowledgement, embracing and breathing, letting go and compassion, relief and trust. Be gentle with yourself and let these feelings sink deep into your gypsy spirit. Begin to see yourself flowing through life as a gypsy—happy, fulfilled, and having an attitude of gratitude. I dare say—sooner rather than later—gratitude will exude from you like a shimmering light. This light will grow and multiply, and with it, you will begin shedding the darkness in your life, allowing you to feel lighter and more comfortable in your gypsy skin.

There are many ways to embrace and express thankfulness. For me, I add it to my yoga practice as I set my intention. When I make my fermented foods I blow it a kiss and say kind words, (yes I talk and give gratitude to my food) and I can be heard multiple times a day asking my children what they are thankful for.

Action Exercise:

1. Write down 3 things each morning when you wake up that you are thankful for. Think about them each for a minute and really feel the thankfulness run through your veins.

    - _____
    - _____
    - _____

2. Get a dedicated "Thankful Journal" for yourself. Any notebook can do, just make sure to use it consistently.
3. Find a song that exemplifies what thankfulness means to you and play it each morning as a part of your morning routine.
4. List 3 ideas: (Example: Grateful by Brotha James.)

    1. _____
    2. _____
    3. _____

5. Ask your children, family or friends what brings them the most joy, and allow them to help inspire you.

The people in your life that you are drawn to are grateful. The people who shine brightly, and are so happy, are grateful. Our forefathers, and the great authors throughout history, were grateful. By harnessing an attitude of gratitude each and every day, you too will become grateful.

Action Game:

- As you get dressed in the morning, before you put on your bra or panties, make sure you put on your gratitude. Can you imagine if all of us who lacked gratitude for our lives did not get to wear a bra to work? Take this image with you and don't forget to wear gratitude.

- First thing in the morning as you brush your teeth, write in lipstick on your mirror one thing that you love about your life! As you wipe it off and brush one more time before retiring to bed, fill your body with gratitude for that one little aspect of your life. As you sleep, that gratefulness will permeate throughout your very soul, preparing you to feel an even deeper sense of gratitude tomorrow.

You are welcomed to pick and choose the tools that resonate with you the most. You know you best, and life is an evolution, so choose how you like to work on your thankfulness muscle!

By working on your thankfulness muscle every day, you will begin to see your life and the world in a new light. You will begin to notice the magical simple things in life, which before seemed meaningless. The insignificant, become significant! Concentrate on looking for the tiny sparks in your life. Once ignited with thankfulness, make way for pure abundance.

Thankful people are warm, inviting, and you want to be near them. Be near them and become that person that everyone wants to hug. Get out in life, meet people, bless others' lives through your thankful attitude, and see all that the Universe gives back to you.

For more tips, go to www.GypsyFam.com/GypsyLivingTips

What inspires gratitude within your soul?

_____

_____

_____

_____

_____

_____

_____

_____

_____

_____

_____

_____

_____

_____

Who inspires a thankful attitude in your world?

_____

_____

_____

_____

_____

_____

_____

_____

_____

_____

_____

_____

_____

_____

DOODLE PAGE

IV

"Y" is for yes

"Yes is an energetic place. When you're coming from this energy, it alters and impacts the way you see yourself, your life, your thoughts, and your feelings. It shapes your actions right here in the present moment. When being a yes, you're someone who is standing positively for what's happening in your life and for what you want to have happen in your future—you're a person who's up to something bigger. Yes sets the stage for being of power."

—BARON BAPTISTE

Say Yes to all things good In Your energy creating!

A gypsy says "yes" and she is up for almost anything! She sees the fun in life and welcomes adventure in the unknown. She jumps into the mystery with wild abandon *and* a sensible awareness that life gives us what we believe it will.

You may have heard a saying relating to "whatever we seek we find." If we seek from darkness and narrowmindedness, that is what will show up in our lives. On the other hand, as soon as we shift our thinking to the light, abundance, and consciousness, guess what happens? You have the option to adopt the attitude that good people, situations, and circumstances always show up for you. Right now, you have the choice to believe that is 100% true. If you are already fighting this belief, then it's time to face the music and realize that you are fighting yourself, which will only keep you in a place of despair. It is a hard fact to face, but facing it is exactly what will set you free. It is time to move on, get out of it, and be a "yes" person for you.

Since I converse with my children about this topic on a regular basis, I find that while writing about it, it helps me to picture their faces and imagine what I would say to them. It goes something like this...

Hello my beautiful goddess of light,
I see today that you are struggling with spite.
Some darkness inside that I sense is the cause,
of something so precious that it beckons us pause.
My dear one whatever we seek we shall find,
so I am curious what has you entrapped in such a bind?
For when something inside of us causes us grief,
we needn't look further than ourselves, as we're chief.
We are the master of our own ship,
we are our very own queen of the night.
And in these truths we know that the fight,
is not really about them, that, he, she or me,
it is just something happening inside the sea.
The sea of emotion that rages inside,
some call it ego, selfishness or pride.
But they would be wrong my dear sweet little one.
For inside I know that within you the battle is won,
of all goodness and love you have a ton.

You are already worthy of all the love, success
and abundance the Universe has to share,
it is all yours my darling if you but care to dare.
Dare to know all that is out there for you,
care to breathe life in and let go of the blue.
I know all of this is out there for you,
so breathe in life deep, let go of outcome,
for you my angel, and are an endless fountain.
A fountain of youth, of love and of yes,
so learn to smile, breathe and let go of stress.
Everything you need, you already embrace,
so move through life's trials with ease and grace.
Knowing you are enough, worthy and complete,
now venture off, go! You command the fleet.

I know you love and give to others with an open heart. I also know that this has likely left you feeling hurt more often times than not. It is with so much love that I ask you to say "yes."

Please heed this warning: be a yes person for you.

The demon you must watch for is Yes to Everything. If you are like me, this is difficult for you to swallow, as it can seem contradictory. Yet, this is a simple life-changing concept.

If you are saying "yes" to everything in life, then you are most likely very unhappy because being a yes person does not mean you actually say "yes" to everything and everyone. If you do that, you will be saying "no" to that which is most important to you. The more you say "yes" to what you *do* want, the more you will be okay with saying "no" to things, people, and circumstances that *don't* align with your gypsy spirit.

I know this may sound backwards. I still remember the first time I heard, "say no" and I felt enormous opposition inside because it was easier for me to say "yes" to others and "no" to myself. It was easier to give others my time and attention and not think about what I wanted. I played this trick with myself for years because it is easier to give, serve, and say "yes" to others than it is to ourselves. Why? I believe this is engrained in us during our childhood through family dynamics and birth order, as well as, our religious and cultural influences. Depending on our circumstances, many of these aspects usually play a huge role in our beliefs about whether we should say "yes" to others over our own needs or wishes.

The mental game I suggest using to reverse this begins with you saying "no" to everything and everyone. Afterwards, if you'd like, take time to think about the request and decide if you actually want to do it. Then, you can reply and say, "You know I actually do have time for that, I would be happy to."

This way, people won't take advantage of your time because you are demonstrating that you are in charge of your life. By giving yourself ample time to think about your priorities, you alone determine if the request is worthy of your time and attention. If it is, you can give your "yes" appropriately, in line with your authentic wishes.

What I have learned is that when you say "yes" to activities that don't fully align with your dreams and desires, you are saying "yes" to the creation of negative energy within yourself. This negative energy becomes a time and energy-sucking vampire because when you say "yes" to someone else but don't want to, you are sacrificing your own happiness, even your very own dreams.

Welcome to living like a gypsy, where you can say "no" with a smile! You literally can say "no" while giving a hug at the same time, even with words of encouragement. With this approach, you can actually empower the people you say "no" to and they will feel your love and positive energy. You have the ability to teach others how to be a gypsy spirit goddess who values her time and energy, and prioritizes her dreams. It is not personal or emotional; it is simply because you are saying "yes" to you, first and foremost. Think of how many other gypsies you can teach through the unending ripples that this one beautiful truth can exponentially reach.

Take a quiet moment to think about the times that you say "yes." Do you believe you are showing that person that you love, honor, and support them? Adversely, when you say "no" are you really saying to that person that they are not worthy of your time and attention? This belief is merely a symptom of the problem, which is that you are attaching the words "yes" and "no" to your emotions, and most likely an expectation that you feel is placed on you. Offer yes's for you. When you say "yes" to yourself, everything and everyone else in your life will begin to fall into place.

Being a yes person is something that comes too easy for me as well. I used to be one of those women that said "yes" to opportunity, vision, and potential. The problem was that I said "yes" to the opportunities of others. In short, I gave up my power.

For a time, I was unhappy and would wake up in the middle of the night with panic attacks, which I had never experienced before. Upon waking, a thought would pop into my mind, my heart would race, and I was filled with anxiety and panic. All because I was going against my own yes's and giving my power to another. My body and mind could not handle it and I was in constant turmoil simply because I had said "yes" to someone else instead of myself. As soon as I realized this and made the necessary adjustments, all was well. It may surprise you how easy it can be to get back on track. Your gypsy sprit wants to say "yes" to you, so do it!

Have you ever noticed that we all tell ourselves stories? It's like we all have a play going on inside our head where we give the people in our lives specific roles to play. On a much deeper level, when we say "yes" to others above ourselves it is because we do not feel worthy of what we want. In short, you do not feel good enough to make yourself the top priority. Even with kids and a career, you *can* and *must* put yourself first. This is not selfish, this is the truth, and once you accept it, your life and your gypsy spirit will begin to feel awake, empowered, and ready to be unleashed. I encourage you to let this sink in and to think about why and to whom you say "yes."

Action Exercises:

- Make a list of 5-10 people you say "yes" to above yourself. (Note: If you have children, they may be on the list.)

  1. _____
  2. _____
  3. _____

4. _____

5. _____

6. _____

7. _____

8. _____

9. _____

10. _____

- Make a list of *why* you say "yes" to them above yourself.

_____

_____

_____

_____

_____

- Make a list of the 3 most frustrating, time sucking activities in your life.

    1. _____

    2. _____

    3. _____

- Make a list of the top 3 priorities in your life.

    1. _____

    2. _____

    3. _____

- Write down the one thing you want to do more than anything else. Something you have always dreamed about doing.

    1. _____

- Explore your relationship with your parents, how did they value you?

  _____

  _____

- Make a list of 3 activities you naturally say "yes" to.
  1. _____
  2. _____
  3. _____

- Make a list of 3 activities that would encourage you to say "yes" to yourself more often.
  1. _____
  2. _____
  3. _____

- Make a list of 3 activities you will do on a daily basis which will ensure you keep making yourself a priority.
  1. _____
  2. _____
  3. _____

- Make a list of 3 reasons you are worthy of saying "yes" to.
  1. _____
  2. _____
  3. _____

Your gypsy spirit has many layers and all that you have to do to unravel them is to be *willing to go into the hurt, pain, and false beliefs and shed them*. By throwing them out, you will begin to live for you. This is the most powerful gift I can share with you, but only *you* can acknowledge and honor your value and worth.

When I was uncovering these layers and discovering my gypsy spirit, I used bits and pieces of guidance from many different books. My goal is to offer you all of the tools that helped me combined within this one book. Remember, this is a very personal journey. However, if you feel that you need assistance, as I did, that is okay too.

Your spouse or someone close to you *may* be able to assist, however, more times than not, they are not the best person to help. This is a process and it does not happen overnight, which can be extremely frustrating for the person watching their loved one go through a challenge. It is human nature to want to step in with an answer, so allowing a loved one to follow their own road takes patience and persistence.

Because of this reason, I have created a guide program.

You are not alone. There are many suffering with the same issues you are. Our guide program is designed to support you on this journey, should you need us.

A note about abusive relationships. Do NOT tolerate them, ever, for any reason. You are worthy of living in a relationship that serves the best parts of you, 100%. Abusive relationships happen when a person is fearful of unleashing their gypsy spirit. If you value yourself, you will never let anyone abuse you in any way. No gypsy stays in a relationship that does not serve his or her highest good. My community is here for anyone in this situation. There is a free guidance video for anyone involved in an abusive relationship at www. gypsyfam.com/gypsytips.

DOODLE PAGE

V

"P" is for positive purpose

*"If you can't figure out your purpose, figure
out your passion. For your passion will
lead you right into your purpose."*

—BISHOP T.D. JAKES

POSITIVE PURPOSE IS THE INTENT IN ALL WE DO

Positive purpose surpasses simply having a passion for
something. It runs much deeper, aligning you with your
life's destiny and mission. Do you know *your* purpose on
Earth? Do you know why you are here at this time, in this
place, with these circumstances? I hope that inside your
fire is being stoked, the eye of the storm is building, and
your passion is turning from a dull pink to a vibrant red!
If not, don't worry, it isn't as hard as you think once you
set an intention to connect to it. Stay open, breathe, and
allow yourself to connect with your inner gypsy spirit as we
continue to go a level deeper into positive purpose.

The world needs more people that are passionate,
however, we must go a step beyond passion, for when we

live passionately we are like a ship in a storm without a compass. I figured out the hard way that passion alone is not enough. One day, I found my passion had run out and it felt as if my insides had become battered and hardened. While passion is wonderful, it is not sustaining. I wrote this poem, initially thinking of my past when I realized how many of us fall into this trap. If you have lived passionately and have been hurt in some way, there is hope and understanding. Maybe you can relate.

Passionate people! You energy balls!
You have lived with zeal and zest, and will inevitably fall.
But in this fall, worry not, all will be well,
for one of life's greatest lessons, I will now tell.
Life with passion seemingly surpasses all,
for a time, it is enough, until you hit the wall.
So be careful for passion can turn on a dime,
it will drive you and thrill you and keep you for a time.
Until one day it will seem not enough,
your skill and talents, maybe you're not quite so tough.
And then one day you will fall down and wonder,
what has all this been for? Was it all just a blunder?
And slowly you will begin to learn,
more about you, and life's true purpose you'll turn.
You will begin to harness life's greatest lesson,
no need to grab a Smith & Wesson.
Although the pit of despair is deep,
for those who are unwilling to walk as sheep.
The pit and the depth, shows us we are just human,
no need to despair there is no show called Truman.
For all that you lacked, was a deeper meaning,
I know that you felt it, think of it as
part of your mortal cleaning.
Positive purpose brings meaning to life,

passion can leave us with anger and strife.
So recognize all as a part of the plan,
of becoming the best you that you possibly can.
Your life's experiences are the perfect prescription,
one in which years ago would have read like encryption.
And now you can see that the highs and the lows,
were not really life's box in the ring blows.
They were simply your teachers for life's greater meaning,
the true test of time is those who endure life's screening.
For a life full of purpose is a purposeful life,
those words now have meaning because of the knife.
The knives of life you endured seemed sharp at the time,
but look back on it now, it's all just a rhyme.
You have chosen to live a life fuller of purpose,
embrace who you are, and live life to the fullest.

For years, I thought the capital "P" stood for passion. And although I would say I am a passionate person, it is my positive purpose that keeps me aligned with my destiny. Why? Having passion is very singular. It is you or me. We likely say, "Oh yes, she is a very passionate person!" This is how we define or describe some individuals. On the other hand, positive purpose is when we work together as a team. Purpose is much larger and grander than passion because it brings people (gypsies) together for a common goal, vision, or purpose.

I experienced this as I dove head first into fitness after my eight-year career in the mortgage industry ended in 2008. It had served my family and I well, but ultimately it was not fulfilling for me. One day at the gym one of the fitness instructors asked me if I had heard of Zumba ™ Fitness. I had not. She said, "You ought to try it. You would like it and would we be really good at it." That was all the encouragement I needed. A month later, there happened to be a training at the gym I was attending so I decided to give it a try. Although I had not been to one class ever, she was right, I was good at it. Something inside of me sparked to life and I felt an instant passion for it.

Although it took me a few weeks of non-stop practicing, it became clear that leading others by being a physical example was something I had a knack for. A few months later, we opened a fitness business called The Warehouse in Southern Utah. The stage and lighting was the perfect atmosphere for our classes, and within a few months, I had 70-100 students, five days a week. For the next two years, I ran a flourishing fitness business, improved my skills, added fitness certifications to my resume, taught new formats, and dreamed bigger than I ever had before.

When we sold the business and moved to South Carolina, Zumba ™ Fitness hired me as a choreography specialist (aka Zumba Jammer ™ or ZJ). I hit the ground running as soon as we arrived in South Carolina, not wasting a minute. In retrospect, that was hard on me. Instead of relaxing and feeling my way through this next phase of my life, I moved through it relying on passion alone. For a while, passion took me all over the world teaching my choreography. It also pushed me to make phone call after phone call, and answer Facebook message after message. After a while, promoting my sessions and classes as a ZJ as well as teaching on a weekly basis in my hometown began to drive me crazy. Not to mention, on top of that, we opened another fitness business, against our better judgement.

After a year and a half, I was totally burnt out. I had traveled to Switzerland, Puerto Rico, and all over the East Coast teaching and dancing. At the time, it didn't occur to me that I was giving my power away to very specific dreams instead of letting my life unfold by staying connected to my gypsy spirit.

Eventually, we moved to Arlington, Virginia. This is where I also began my career as a Vitamix representative. This was a pinnacle point in my life. I was amazed at how much income you could make by selling a blender! I was a natural, but it was hard work...really hard work. Long days, filled with hairnets, plastic gloves, food preparation, and setting up and tearing down. Not to mention the endless flow of people, some who wanted to engage with you and some that did not. Others just wanted the free little white cup filled with the delicious goodness. It was exhausting. Sometimes, I would wake up in the middle of the night because my hands were tingling from the all-day use of the tamper stick! I endured this grueling schedule for one reason—I wanted to learn the art of selling. It was crucial for me to learn how to disconnect people's responses from my emotions. In other words, this was more than a way to make money; I was on a mission to improve my talents and myself. This lasted for six months. Little did I know just how six short months would bridge my fitness career to a place of deeper connection and fulfillment.

It was at this point in my life that a book called *The Miracle Morning* showed up on my doorstep. I had no idea where it came from until I read the name Jon Berghoff (head of the Vitamix reps at the time). This book gave me the courage to resign as a ZJ and Vitamix representative, and focus on creating my own HIIT workout, RAW. I began to feel free. This was the beginning of a new chapter of my life.

As I said "yes" to activities that I loved, over time I became a presenter at conferences. I credit a large part of this to my willingness to say "yes" to me and the things I love (like working out). I moved people physically so they were ready and open to be moved emotionally. For me, this is beauty at its best. This manifestation took eight years, and maybe a lifetime of preparation. By following my gypsy spirit, I found myself in the right place at the right time, with the right people.

In retrospect, it is easy for me to see how it all connected to become my life's purpose, but the previous stories were not the end, nor the beginning. I would quit as a ZJ, launch my own online fitness program, move back to Southern Utah with my family, open and close another fitness business, and repackage and sell a trampoline business. Finally, after all of that, I let all of my passions and old dreams go. I had to. Emotionally, I was holding on so tight and pushing so hard that it was breaking me. (Sometimes the fitness industry can do that to a person).

Afterwards, I took a three-year introspective journey into healing myself. Through my long adored practice of yoga, spirituality, and discovering my truth, my true healing began. Yoga has been a foundational tool in my life for over two decades. During this time, I became certified (level 1 and 2) in WINGS energy work and began to learn and master gut healing through fermentation.

What led me to discovering this purpose? I longed for a deeper connection and meaning. It took me a long time to realize that much of my frustration stemmed from not understanding this about myself. When you live life with zest there is usually something you desire, something bigger. Maybe it is a dream or a goal. When you do not have the whole map laid out, (nobody does) there is bound to be some bumps and bruises along the way. What I realized about my journey is that my passion only got me so far. However, since I did not know what I did not know at the time, what could I have done differently to make my journey more purposeful? Nothing.

My passion helped lead me to my purpose; it just took longer than I wanted. Although we do not get to choose when and how we learn lessons in life, we do get to make hundreds of tiny choices on a daily basis. Each decision is made with either an abundance mindset or a mindset of lack. Looking back, I would not have made any decisions differently, because I know each one led me to become aligned with my gypsy spirit. The biggest lesson I learned was to trust and let go of the outcome. If only I had known then what I know now, it would have relieved a lot of stress. What I failed to see then was the pattern in my life surrounding broken agreements.

Remember, passion is not enough, but it will get you through to the next step. The step where you gain clarity in your life. Many times, it takes prior life experience to understand exactly what you are seeking. Experiences offer us knowledge and awareness, which we can add to our bank of intuition to pull from the next time we make a decision. Therefore, the more we have to pull from, the better! Maybe you do not know what you want or where you want to go. If you lack experience, is it any wonder that you lack direction and purpose?

Look at it like this, the past is a bridge to teach you how to live with purpose in your present moments. Passion will temporarily bridge the gap between purpose, talents, and fulfillment. You will know it when it happens so all that you have to do is live with an open heart. By doing more of what you love and staying aligned with your gypsy spirit, you will smile more and struggle less.

Visualize a gypsy in the forest. She is laughing and appears to be dancing alone, confident in herself. However, she never travels alone. She is always cognizant of others and the impact she has on them and them on her. She is a part of a greater purpose and plan, recognizing that she is a creator and when she joins others, that creative energy magnifies throughout the universe.

The enemy of positive purpose is selfishness and **ego**. The ego driven person is one that ends up alone. You see ego in the one that jumped into the caravan driven by her own beauty and excellence. She is the one who danced on the stage simply to hear the claps and admiration from the spectators. She craved this to cover up some insecurity and to help convince herself how amazing she is because she can't see it. She is full of passion for herself and what she wants, determined to shine. And shine she does, for a time until she looks around and realizes that her once surrounding gypsy family is gone. She didn't recognize that her pride blocked the call to leave for the journey along with everyone else. Now she is left alone on the stage that once seemed so joyous, with a feeling of emptiness sweeping over her. The lights, music, and spectators are gone and she is standing alone in the cold rain. Her passion drains out of her along with the raindrops that fall from the tips of her curly hair into the dark trampled earth. She feels completely alone.

We are all on a journey and I believe that passion is a big part of that journey. I would agree that passion is an essential aspect of life, but I also believe that when that passion meets positive purpose, a completely new energy force for good is created. Why? Because others will feel your passion and want to be a part of the movement. When we have leaders who are visionaries, willing to push the envelope and create new paths, life is elevated.

Elevate your passion. Elevate your life. Allow your purpose to find you and embrace positive intention as the governing choice. If you are lost, don't worry; keep reading this book over and over. I promise each time you do, a layer will shed and your gypsy spirit will open more. Let the deeper meaning of my words connect with you and one day soon, your path and purpose will become clearer.

Action Exercise:

- List 3 things you love to do.
    1._____
    2._____
    3._____

- List 3 things you would do if you had all the time in the world.
    1._____
    2._____
    3._____

- List 3 things you would do if money, a job, and a family were not an issue.
    1._____
    2._____
    3._____

- List 3 times you have tried and failed at something you were passionate about. (Note: if you have not failed, you have not tried. We will get into this up ahead).
  1._____
  2._____
  3._____

- List 3 ideas about what your purpose could potentially be.
  1._____
  2._____
  3._____

Hey, I know making lists is time consuming and it possibly forces you to feel a bit uncomfortable. That is good; it means you are making progress! Stop now and do the above exercises if you haven't already! You must face the greatness inside of you...it is waiting for you.

DOODLE PAGE

VI

"S" is for self-love

*"What lies behind us and what lies before us are
tiny matters compared to what lies within us."*

—RALPH WALDO EMERSON

SELF-LOVE ENCOMPASSES THE LIMITLESS CONFIDENCE WE HAVE
WITHIN OUR SOULS FOR SELF-EXPRESSION

Self. The self. You. Your inner goddess. Your soul. Your "it."
Your spice. Your jam. Your magical essence. Your touch,
your eyes, your smell, and your embrace. In summation,
your gypsy spirit. The quest to unleash your inner gypsy
comes with the awareness of your very own deep-rooted
sense of self-love. Learning to love yourself in a meaningful
and fulfilling way that breeds confidence and worthiness
is imperative. You are now going to develop a personal
relationship with yourself. Gypsies of the world, it is time
to rise up and recognize that you are enough!

What does this really mean? What is self-love? We hear
about it, people write and talk about it, but to feel self-love
is quite another phenomenon. I like to describe self-love

simply by conveying it as the way you feel about yourself when no one is around. The voice in your head when you look in the mirror. Are you naturally self-critical?

Of course you are, and probably your own worst critic as well. This happens because internally you are judging yourself over and over again. There is an internal battle taking place in your mind and spirit. At times, you overcome it and feel as though you have moved past or mastered this voice. You may be surprised to hear me say, the fact is the voice never goes away. You must learn how to let those voices go, and choose to listen to the other voices—the positive ones. Those voices are not you. One of the best books I have found on this subject is called, *The Untethered Soul,* by Michael A. Singer. He explains that you must be willing to embrace all voices, without running from any one of them. Simply by noticing and consciously choosing to listen to the voices that empower and embrace your gypsy spirit, it becomes easier to let everything else go.

To recognize the distinction between embracing and running is simple when you ask yourself—is there bitterness? If you have bitterness and negative emotions surrounding the way you feel about yourself in any way, you are not being honest with yourself. It is imperative to face this in order to unleash your gypsy spirit's self-love.

Action Exercise:

- What would you change about yourself?

  _____

  _____

  _____

  _____

  _____

- What do you dislike about yourself?

  _____

  _____

  _____

  _____

  _____

- What are you critical of about yourself?

  _____

  _____

  _____

  _____

  _____

- Can you pinpoint when you began feeling this way?

  _____

  _____

  _____

  _____

  _____

- Was there a specific circumstance?

  _____

  _____

  _____

_____

_____

- Who was involved?

  _____

  _____

  _____

  _____

  _____

- If necessary, can you address your feelings with someone who was involved?

  _____

  _____

  _____

  _____

  _____

- What is the one thing you can resolve in your life so that you have peace in your body, mind, and spirit?

  _____

  _____

  _____

  _____

  _____

- Take a deep breath.
- If there are people that you need to address to let this go, do it today. Call, text, or email and find a resolution.

  _____

  _____

  _____

  _____

  _____

- Now we will go into a vocal expression of love and worthiness.

Action Exercise:

To preface, you may feel silly and maybe even a little crazy while doing this exercise. Just know that this is totally normal. (Although it is important to remind yourself that nothing and no one is "normal.")

Deep breath.

There you go, let yourself feel cool with this strange, yet satisfying exercise.

1. Say-*I am worthy.*
2. Yell-*I am worthy!*
3. Say-*I am enough.*
4. Yell-*I am enough!*
5. Say-*I am beautiful.*
6. Yell-*I am beautiful!*
7. Say-*my body is beautiful.*
8. Yell-*my body is beautiful!*
9. Say-*I have everything I need right now to live the life I want.*
10. Yell-*I have everything I need right now to live the life I want and I am enough!*

Did you feel totally silly or powerful? I now recommend repeating the exercise. This time pause for 5 seconds between each one (it will seem like an eternity). At first you may feel as though you are convincing yourself. Soon these words will empower you and you will know they are true.

Grab a mirror. Now keep your eyes focused on yourself in the mirror. Notice what is coming up for you. What feelings are being awakened deep within? Are you being critical? If so, don't resist it just allow those thoughts to come and go. Let it continue to move through you and right out of your mind. Now, just be.

Action Exercise:

> Write down how this experience was for you. Write about what came up for you. Share it with a friend, just let them know this is an important exercise in the book you are reading or listening too. You never know whose angel of the day you may be. Millions need these words. Be a force for good in sharing what is working for you.

_____

_____

_____

_____

_____

_____

_____

_____

_____

Self-love is a topic that is crucial for you to understand. It may be a delicate subject for you, but know that you are not alone. Sadly, a lack of self-love is most people's natural state in our culture. Shifting the focus to analyzing and bettering yourself can be something that is uncomfortable. Nevertheless, I know it is possible for you to develop this love for yourself, right here and right now through a few easy steps.

Action Exercise:

- Acknowledge that self-love is needed.
- Recognize your actions that deflect your love of self and others.
- Go into your heart and feel love for how inherently wonderful you are.
- Breathe and let go of the past, be compassionate about your current path, and commit to a new way of being.

Self-love includes being kind and giving to yourself, while also encompassing much of the high frequency inherent in these words: abundance, worthiness, and divinity. Positive high frequencies are extremely powerful and their energy hangs around. Unfortunately, guilt and shame are also high frequency words, however, in a negative context. I believe that if you are anything like me, you are very heart-centered, possessing huge potential to love others. While that is a wonderful trait, it is of utmost important to focus on yourself first.

Have you ever put others above yourself? I would bet you have. Do you have a belief that you must give and serve others, even at the cost of losing yourself? This selflessness is not a positive attribute as many of us are taught, but instead a wonderful recipe for unhappiness. Doing for others what you won't do for yourself is no longer acceptable when living in line with your gypsy spirit. Giving love is wonderful, but it is critical that you learn to harness the ability to love yourself first. When you brush over this concept and forget yourself, in essence you choose to forget the greatness of your gypsy spirit.

What does it teach your friends, family, and children when you discount yourself? Many people are struggling in today's world, leading them to self-medicate their sadness, loneliness, and depression. Our purpose in life is not to feel lost and lonely, while using substances to simply "make it through."

Stop for a minute, take a breath, and realize that your lack of self-love is quite possibly a serious aspect of your unhappiness. Although you washed away your lack of worthiness when you jumped into our magical pond in chapter two, that was just the beginning. It was a great start, however, without bringing full awareness to your thoughts, patterns, and behaviors, and implementing the action tools, you very well may fall back into the trap of self-less giving.

The intent of the following poem is to help heal the insecurities that need to be healed in you at this time. You have the power to do that by allowing my words to assist you right here and now. All that you have to do is allow them in, and allow yourself to be healed. This is the beginning of you moving into a future full of bright hope.

You Are

A goddess of beauty, a star in the night,
a queen of all good, of greatness and light.
No matter if you put on a good front,
deep down in your soul you have taken the brunt.
A dash of guilt, a spoonful of shame,
sure will go nicely when you've thought of your name.
Your mind in the past has been a source of the pains,
now let us renew, rebuild and reclaim.
For all that you need IS to feel how worthy you are,
now look in the mirror YOU needn't go far.
There's a call that reminds us to thine own self be true,

you are loved, now love you and
share with others this clue.
To see you are special, loved and so good,
of this self-love embrace and let go of all should's.
So here, now and forever let it always be known,
that you are enough, much courage you've shown.
You are here now complete imperfectly you,
embrace yourself and smile and be made anew.
Each day as you rise be sure to remember,
that each roaring fire begins with an ember.

The demon of self-love is guilt. Guilt is the deep dark internal hole that grows deeper each time you believe you have done something wrong. It is quite possibly the most powerless feelings on earth and goes right along with shame. The string of pearls full of wisdom that we are threading will snap and cascade down across the floor if you continue to entertain thoughts of guilt and shame. Guilt, shame, and unworthiness are negative high frequency words as I mentioned above. They have the ability to swirl around you like a deep thick fog. Once you invite them in, they can be difficult to release. Guilt is an untrue story that we tell ourselves which consistently brings what we *don't* want into our world. Sadly, because it feels so familiar, we find comfort there. We learn at a young age to buy into the story of guilt. We tend to believe the stories that our parents tell themselves, eventually taking them on as our truths. However, it's not the real truth, but instead just the one you tell yourself is true. You have the option right now to recognize that you have been buying into this sorrowful story, but you also have the power to choose what to believe moving forward.

You have learned about life through your experiences. In the midst of them, you ultimately decided what *is* and *isn't* possible. Strangely enough, we tend to build restrictions and borders around our lives early on, holding fast to those limiting views of what is possible.

It has been my experience that organized religion can further foster feelings of guilt and self-doubt.

I was raised in an incredibly intense cultural religion called the LDS, Latter Day Saints, or probably most popularly known as—Mormons. No, I was not raised in one of the modern offshoot polygamous sects, however, that *was* a belief that the church practiced until they outlawed it in the 1890's. Some still believe they will practice this again one day in heaven.

As a child, I never questioned the church's teachings verbally, although I did so internally. I was pretty easy-going and followed the many rules that were considered the "right" behaviors because I never wanted to step outside of the bubble. As I grew into a young adulthood, outsiders wanted to know who I was and what I was about. This made me question my beliefs and led me on a journey of consciously contemplating what *I* wanted for *my* life.

I decided to take ownership of my path after figuring out that I wanted a life that looked much different than the one I grew up in. Although I was sure it would be different, I didn't even know what that looked like! The good part was that I was okay with the mystery of the unknown and letting go of the outcome.

Over the next few years, I internally battled for self-understanding. Although I felt this was a choice that was true to my heart, there was a disconnect from my head and the decades of teachings, as well as, the perceived cultural pressures. This did not resolve overnight. I was not strong enough to leave my upbringing behind right away. It took me many years to finally do so.

Even after I met my husband, Charles, and was sure about wanting a life with him, I was still plagued with feelings of helplessness and indecision about what was best for me. I was still too concerned with what others would think and say if I did not marry a church member and remain active.

For me, being raised as a Mormon brought so much goodness into my life by offering me a strong sense of community and family. However, it also caused me a great deal of hardship, guilt, and dissention between my family and my own gypsy spirit. Religion can be a source of power and light for many, and I have great reverence for that, yet I believe that religion also has the ability to negatively affect and confuse our simple spirits.

Obviously, life is more complicated than choosing between right and wrong. Mistakes, or what I like to think of as learning experiences, are meant to be made. More times than not, life is messy and full of ups and downs. After years of working to understand my emotions, I decided to share my story of leaving the religion in a poem on my blog. As I verbalized my feelings, I realized I had so much to say on the topic so my husband encouraged me to write a separate book about it.

While I do not think it is good to concentrate on negativity, I do believe that it is important for me to be honest about my experience, especially if it helps others. Why should we hide who we are and what we believe from those we love? Can we not have a common respect for each other and our differences? My intent with my upcoming book on this subject is to help others come to an understanding, peace, and acceptance about their own journey. These feelings are found in organized religion, body image, parental expectations and more.

I am not one for holding onto bitterness and anger. Quite the opposite. I see my journey as a necessary one that helped me become who I am today. However, looking back, I do believe that I could have been more confident earlier on in my life and marriage, which would have led to many years where I didn't suffer with guilt and shame. Not for what I have done or how I have chosen to live, but for thinking those that I love would not like me if I was not a part of the religion. Isn't that silly?

If this subject is intriguing to you, and you would like to learn more about my experience you can visit www.gypsyfam. com/blog. It is titled, *MY POEM. MORMONISM.*

It is important for me to reiterate that I understand that being a part of an organized religion works for many people. I want you to know, from the bottom of my heart, that I honor and respect your journey, as you probably honor and respect mine. We all need love and acceptance, and if your religious beliefs help you do that for yourself and others, that makes me smile and warms my heart.

If you find that being a part of a religion does not lift you up and you are merely doing it because of pressure from yourself or others, it is possible this is a part of why you have become cynical and unhappy. This is an important distinction for you to make as the paradigm you have been living by is no longer working for you. I encourage you to make a change for *you*. Your life and happiness depends on your belief that you are worthy of everything that you desire. We all find this in different ways and call it by different names, and in all its forms is beautifully abundant to me.

Many negative emotions can block us from fully embracing love for ourselves. Another one is the feeling of inadequacy, which can ripple through our minds, stunting our growth in developing self-love. There is no question; this is too high a price to pay. Your gypsy spirit is ready and waiting for you to rise. So, rise up! You are good enough right now. You are exactly who you need to be in each moment of every circumstance. You are exactly who you need to be. Life is the greatest mystery of all and a gypsy sees hers for what it is—the greatest journey ever—that is meant to be thoroughly enjoyed.

Life can only be enjoyed at the deepest level when you are present to your own worth. In simple terms, you must love yourself first, only then can you love others. If I may digress a bit and acknowledge the fact that, there are those of us who needed to feel love from another first to fully understand how to do it for ourselves. Although I was confident, I did not love myself. It wasn't until I experienced Charles's unconditional love for me that I began to shed the skin of self-unworthiness. If you can relate, I will happily be that person for you should you need me to be. I am here for you, I love you, I respect you, and I honor your journey and willingness to allow me to be a part of your healing and the unleashing of your gypsy spirit!

Your life is waiting for you. This one-step is critically important and it is time for you to move forward through this phase of life so you can begin to live your life as a gypsy, full of abundance in each and every aspect of your life.

Action Exercise:

Write down any feelings or thoughts that are coming up for you about your self-love or lack thereof:

_____

_____

_____

_____

_____

_____

_____

_____

_____

_____

Action Exercise:

- Begin each day by looking in the mirror and feeling love for yourself. Once you feel it, you can expand it to those you surround yourself with.
- Bed option - Cross your arms in front of you, hold onto opposite shoulders, and gently bow your head. This instantly connects you to the universal healing power.
- When a self-love demon comes up turn on your favorite song and shift your focus.

- What three take-aways from this chapter stand out for you?
    1. _____
    2. _____
    3. _____

- What is your go-to empowerment song? One that makes you happy! Anytime your pearl necklace is about to break, put on your song and get out of your current circumstance and surrounding.
    1. _____
    2. _____
    3. _____

The gypsy living community is here to inspire you, keep you moving forward, and to help connect you with others. As we grow our community, imagine all that you can help others with. Being open and honest with others can also serve you in consistently knowing you are enough and worthy of self-love. Are you a part of the community?

Hop on my website and click on the social media links. Head to Facebook and join our Gypsy Living Community. Leave a comment and introduce yourself.

- List 3 things you can help people with:
    1. _____
    2. _____
    3. _____

- List 3 things you could use a support system for:
    1. _____
    2. _____
    3. _____

DOODLE PAGE

VII

"y" is for young at heart

May we act and live from our child-like heart.
May we feel the freedom of butterfly wings.
May we feel the constant breeze of the power
of the Universe as we swing from the monkey
bars. May we stay young. May we be free. May
we become who we are destined to be.

—ANDREA B. RIGGS

PLAY, DANCE, LAUGH, ENJOY LIFE, AND ALWAYS REMEMBER THAT
YOU ARE ONLY AS OLD AS YOUR HEART, SO KEEP IT YOUNG.

When I think of the happiest people I know, they are playful, happy, and young at heart. For me, the first person that comes to mind is my wonderful mother. Eccentric with a dash of crazy, and a sprinkling of "out there" is just the way I like her. Her spirit laughs and prances around, moving her body freely. Both her and my father are still extremely active and they in their early 70's! While that number may seem quite old, to me, they seem much younger because of how youthful and adventurous their spirits are.

Living with a youthful attitude is *as* important as mastering the ability of letting go of stress and the need to control life's outcomes. If this sounds contradictory, don't worry, later on we will talk more about the importance of how we choose to deal with stress and how it can quite literally lead to the demise of your health.

If you aren't familiar, I would like to point out here that culturally, eastern and western medicine are vastly different. As more of us align with eastern philosophies, many of us are letting go of the western beliefs ingrained in us about health, nutrition and stress. One big difference is that eastern medicine looks at everything as a whole, taking into account the many factors that contribute to our health or dis-ease.

Can the way we view the world around us matter to our health and happiness? It does, more than you may realize. Interpreting our world is the main job of our endocrine system, which is composed of many organs. We have an entire body system that is dedicated to this very concept, how cool is that?

When you look at the world—your career, children, weight loss, and so forth—and feel stress about any or all of those aspects of your life, your body is quite literally analyzing and compensating for the deficits it finds. In short, your body is the battlefield of your thoughts and emotions. Deepak Chopra says, "Instead of this battlefield, let the body be the playground." The way you *feel* about everything in your life matters. Regardless of the words you use to justify those feelings to others, internally you know the truth and therefore, so does your body. Any disease that develops in the body begins with our feelings of dis-ease.

For example, have you noticed some children are maturing at an increased rate? This could be due to family issues, lack of parenting, food and nutrition, social factors, genetics and the like. We have environmental factors as well as internal factors that contribute to abnormalities in our children, adults and the aging population.

What is the drive some of us feel to want to grow up and mature? I recall as a child, I always wanted to grow up faster than I was. I was consumed with getting older so I could be like my three older sisters. I could not wait to go to school, have friends and "hang out" like they did. The future was always exciting to me and I loved spending time planning it! I still remember choosing to stay at home on weekends in high school, while my parents were vacationing in Palm Desert, to plan my college path out so I could be finished via the quickest route possible. It seemed to me that each phase of life was never truly fulfilling because I was always focused on the future and finding the best way to do it more quickly. Contemplating how I could be better prepared for life was always running around my head.

By constantly living in the future, I was not aligned with who I was in the moment. In turn, this blocked me from enjoying my path. I had given up my young-at-heart attitude because I thought growing up would be so wonderful. Being older would be best, right? What I failed to recognize was that my sisters would always be older, and I would always be younger. There was no way to "catch up" to them. While I am now grateful for this fact, it is important to point out that birth order plays a vital role in the way we grow up by continually affecting how we internalize our lives. It is this very concept that describes first daughters with younger siblings as the "caretakers" or "bossy" ones, the middle children more easy-going, and the babies the "spoiled" and dotted over ones. How does that transcend into a youthful attitude? The role you played in your family structure is probably the role you are still playing in your adult life.

Action Exercise:

- Where do you fall in your family?

  _____
  _____
  _____
  _____
  _____

- Did you like it? Why or why not?

  _____
  _____
  _____
  _____
  _____

- What was difficult about your birth order?

  _____
  _____
  _____
  _____
  _____

- What did you like about it?

  _____
  _____
  _____
  _____
  _____

- What have you learned about life from your birth order?

_____

_____

_____

_____

_____

- What beliefs about life would you like to give up that you learned from this family experience?

_____

_____

_____

_____

_____

- What 3 things can you do daily to be more young at heart?
  1. _____
  2. _____
  3. _____

By recognizing how your family treated you and may currently treat you (especially if it is poorly), you can gain the clarity to act out of power instead of complacency. Family is not there to demean or judge, and yet many times, that is exactly what you feel from them. This can be changed simply by you choosing to free yourself from their judgement. Be free and allow your heart to stay young, knowing that those who truly love you will love you no matter what.

There are relationships that serve you and there are those that do not. The key is to understanding the difference between the relationships that serve you and the ones that you love to serve. When you love yourself, you will stand up for yourself and use your voice. Beware: when you use your voice, some people won't like it. It can even make them uncomfortable because they're not used to this new you. Those who don't like your voice may only like to hear themselves talking. If they don't want to hear you, then why are you putting energy into a one-sided relationship?

Why did I want to grow up so badly? What was it about "arriving" at that perfect age, perfect financial place, or perfect life that I was consumed with? What was it about the rat race or living vicariously through my sisters that seemed so intriguing to me? All that I can speculate now is—that is how I interpreted my world. I believed happiness, success, and desire were satisfied sometime in the future, through family, marriage, and a secure future. This is what others modeled for me so I took it on as my own truth, as fictitious as it was. This is also why I had internal disaccord. While all of these are good and many of us want marriage, family and security in our lives, my gypsy spirit felt stifled and confined through this lens.

When you want what others have and give your power to that outcome, you allow yourself to detach from your own life's purpose and forgo living in the present in your own life. This is not living your life; it is walking around as a zombie. This is not ideal, to say the least. In short, I was giving up my power to the image of what I was being taught was "good and right."

Harnessing a youthful heart is a feeling and an attitude. Once you have adopted this attitude, it is life altering. Instead of wanting to grow up and be older and wiser than you are, you choose to be playful and curious like a child. When you maintain your youth, through the awareness that life is simply better when you are more youthful, you let go of the "should" and embrace the "could." This allows you to come from a place of wonderment and child-like awe, learning to dance, laugh, and enjoy life, even the whoopsies! Even when you fall, because you inevitably will, go ahead and get back up because well, you are worth a million times the million whoopsies.

Being playful encompasses resiliency, one of the most important key traits of a gypsy. Gypsies do fail. I'm sure you have failed at something and you will again because we *all* fail. Remember, our failures are an important part of learning and growth. No doubt, you have tried, succeeded, and tried something new and learned from it! This is how a child learns and it is how we, as adults, learn as well. We forget how many mistakes we made as kids and how resilient we were. What makes it even better? When you learn to laugh in the midst of the so-called "failures."

Your youthful attitude will determine the success of your priorities because you must be able to see the sun beyond the clouds. Staying playful with your goals helps your flexibility, enabling you to change course should you need to. It is much easier when you give up the fight of white-knuckling life to be any certain way. Simply, let go of the outcome and your control over what you think it should look like. All that trying to control everything does is cause stress, and the battlefield we talked about earlier. When you choose to live in the flow of life (more about this topic ahead), you will be free.

Gypsies have goals and priorities, as I am sure you do. You may have not known this when you started this book, but you are on your way to understanding life's most important truths. One of those truths is to live fully and laugh at ourselves often. Yes, it is okay to look like a fool and in fact, it is wonderful fun! By embracing this concept, you teach others, especially children, that your ego is not a problem.

It is easy to remember two of a gypsy's favorite things this way...to laugh is to heal and to dance is to release. Did you know that a gypsy loves to dance? This brings me to my next poem about being young at heart.

I once saw a gypsy dancing my way,
she welcomed and smiled at me as if to say,
come dance with me darling and show me your moves,
but inside I knew I hadn't the grooves.
She moved so seamless and so child-like,
I felt so different, like a machine wrapped up tight.
But inside she sparked a youthful desire,
to be careless of worry, she fueled my inner fire.
I took a deep breath, and let go of my fear,
and before I knew it I was crying big tears.
As my body danced, swayed and moved to the beat,
emotion released right down through my feet.
And before I knew it I was having some fun,
gone were the worries and judgments from nuns.
I was dancing and free.
I was laughing with glee.
And all of the sudden, it hit me so quick,
I realized that one of life's greatest tricks,
is the belief that I had about who I must be,
was blinding me so that I could not really see.
I am meant to be free, have fun and enjoy,

I don't need to grow up and become so coy.
I can fail and fall and do my best each day,
for in life's full embrace I will find my own way.
You see my dear friends that gypsy was me,
we all have her near if we are willing to see.

These poems make me so happy! I visualize this scene and something inside me is sparked. What is it? You've probably guessed…my gypsy spirit. I know that when you listen to these poems yours will also be sparked. How do you know? When you giggle inside, maybe shed a tear or even get the chills. The greatness inside of you has been there all along. You do not need to fear it any longer, and for some reason beyond my comprehension, these poems are a key to doing just that.

Life. Many describe this four-letter word as hard, challenging, and difficult. At times, for you and me both, it is true. However, the truth is that you have a choice. You have a choice each time you interpret a situation in your life. Nothing in life has meaning except the meaning you give it. I repeat: nothing in life has meaning, except the meaning *you* give it. Here is another gem of wisdom: whatever you are seeking, you will find. Again, whatever you are focused on looking for, whether that is to be looked down upon, demeaned and abused or lifted up, supported and cherished, you will find it. So begin associating new meaning to life's challenges. Begin to see each challenge in a new, more playful and much less serious manner.

Become childlike and allow yourself the freedom to choose without wrath and judgement. Visualize a child. They are free, lighthearted, and compassionate. Can you think of ways in your life that you could be more compassionate?

Children love to play. In what ways can you play more?

_____
_____
_____

Are there life tasks and priorities that you could make into a fun game? You have the ability to create a new way of life. If you do not, then you cannot expect to see a change. Have you heard Albert Einstein's quote? "Insanity: doing the same thing over and over again and expecting different results."

Action Exercise:

Answer "Yes" or "No"

- Do you accept good things in your life? (Kids do.)

  _____

- Do you allow blessings, support, and advice? (Kids do.)

  _____

- Do you play, dance, and have fun? (Kids do.)

  _____

- Do you go after what you want? (Kids do.)

  _____

Action Exercise:

- What can I do to accept the good things in MY life?

  _____
  _____
  _____
  _____
  _____

- What blessings, support, and advice are coming into MY life?

  _____

  _____

  _____

  _____

  _____

- How do I play, dance, and have fun?

  _____

  _____

  _____

  _____

  _____

- Why is it so easy for ME to go after what I want?

  _____

  _____

  _____

  _____

  _____

The demon of young at heart is _expectation_. How many dreams could have been saved were it not for expectation. The internal bar that you set for others behaviors and actions is a demon in every sense of the word. Without expectation you are forced to see the one person you can control, you. As you let go of expectation and embrace curiosity you will learn to let go of the outcome of your life. By letting go of the way you think your life _must_ be, you create space for what your life _can_ be. For what you are meant to become. This is the only real way to live happily, and it is key to unleashing your gypsy spirit.

Think about your past expectations. Most likely, you have had more than a few expectations that were not met. Whether you were vocal about this or not, internally you were let down. As soon as this road is traveled in the vehicle of expectation, walls go up.

The "walls" are the emotional blocks that prevent our gypsy spirit from being unleashed. These walls morph into anger, bitterness, and many times resentment toward another, or regret from a decision we made.

To have an expectation of another is to give them power to dictate *your* life. In essence, it takes your focus away from what YOU can do, and focuses it on another person. You are asking the question, "What can YOU do for ME?" Do you see how easy it is to give up your power to another?

By giving your power to anyone other than yourself, you abandon your own journey to embrace another's. While this may seem romantic, or temporarily makes you feel safe and secure, it is anything but. Your life is your journey. End of story. By design, you are meant to harness your own personal power, using it to navigate your own journey.

You may not have thought of it this way before, but an expectation is a negative way to look at life. With so many positive ways to view life, we are going to throw this word into the hot magma at the center of the earth. Melt your expectations of self and others in order to unleash your gypsy spirit.

If you do *not* choose to allow your expectations to melt away, you will continue to store those negative emotions, which settle into the very fibers of your being. All of your thoughts and emotions eventually become a part of your DNA. Yes, you my friend are water and empty space full of emotion and energy that can emanate from either positive or negative forces.

Negative stored emotions originate when you felt an emotion that scared you. Not in the Stephen King kind of way, but the visceral way. The fear a child has stemming from being hurt. The fear a woman holds who can't find the strength to stand up for herself to others. The fear that life can't be trusted and the worst fear—that you are not good enough.

If you are feeling it, the fear of confronting harbored emotion is very real. Maybe you do not recognize that you have any fear. You simply see that your shoulders are tight or your lower back has been giving you trouble. Maybe you get headaches or TMJ. Our body is the ultimate machine and will do absolutely anything to survive. It is a master at covering up and looking perfect on the outside. Healers are coming forward and embracing the internal struggle. I believe there is a very good chance you are one of them, or will be soon.

Your struggles most likely stem from expectations you had about life—how you thought your life would be. Maybe about what your husband, boyfriend, or lover would give you. The common denominator in this problem is *you*. The main character in this story is you and the way you choose to look at the world, and internalize relationships. The truth can be hard to face, but it is always worth taking the risk.

It is my belief that the only person you can control is yourself. Therefore, the only one you can have any expectations of is yourself. How then can you learn to become more compassionate with your own expectations?

Action Exercise:

- List 3 current expectations you have of others.
  1. _____
  2. _____
  3. _____

- List 3 current expectations you have of yourself.
  1. _____
  2. _____
  3. _____

- List 3 circumstances where someone has let you down.
  1. _____
  2. _____
  3. _____

- If you removed the expectation, how could the above 3 circumstances turned out differently?
  1. _____
  2. _____
  3. _____

- What could *you* have done differently in that situation?
  1. _____
  2. _____
  3. _____

- Name 3 things you will gain by letting go of expectations of others.
  1. _____
  2. _____
  3. _____

- Why will it be easy for you to let go of expectation?
  1. _____
  2. _____
  3. _____

- What is the price if you do not?
  1. _____
  2. _____
  3. _____

- If you are interested, please visit our Facebook social media group (Gypsy Living Community) and declare 3 ways you can let go of expectation. What are they?
  1. _____
  2. _____
  3. _____

- If you feel moved to do so, share Gypsy Fam-Gypsy Living page with a friend and give one heart felt reason you feel empowered by our work together. Did you do it?

  _____

Expectations take the "heart" out of life, and without the heart you will lose touch with the youthfulness of your gypsy spirit. Expectations have and will continue to douse out flames of passion and desire until the world ends. Expectation is the antithesis to young at heart. After your action exercise, you have a clearer understanding as to why.

Each day you make a choice to live with a pure intent. You can learn from your past challenges and begin to set the priorities of each day by allowing the illusion of expectation to dissipate. This is a muscle and you will strengthen it by adopting a better lens. I will talk about that lens and how important it is in the next chapter.

This is a process and it will take some time to master. Mastery is not the goal—daily improvements is what counts. As such, there are a few rituals I will provide in the upcoming chapters that will serve as a guide for you through your progression. Don't worry, they are fun and practical and found at www.GypsyFam.com/GypsyLivingTips.

Some of these upcoming rituals will challenge you, however they are absolutely worth it. If it doesn't challenge you, it won't change you. We are in the process, right at this very moment, of unleashing your gypsy spirit. This is no small feat. Your life up until this point has been lived through a paradigm. I am offering you the option to adopt a new paradigm to live by.

In order for you to do this, you will need to let go of the old one and dive into the new one. Diving into the new one will be fun and introspective, yet difficult at times. I will ask you to perform simple activities and (while they may seem too simple or silly) they will make a difference in your life. As we go through these life-enhancing activities in the next chapter keep a lookout for that voice in your head that says, "This is too easy, I am not doing that."

Even if you've heard some of the information before, consider this all new information that you are learning for the very first time. It may well be, and even if you have heard some of it, you've never been here with me before. You have never been this age while reading or listening to this book, and absorbing the information from this perspective.

Even if this is your second or third time reading this book, you can go deeper and uncover more and more of yourself. You are meant to evolve, grow, create and to live young at heart.

DOODLE PAGE

PART 2

VIII

planting the gypsy seed

"Without continual growth and progress,
such words as improvement, achievement,
and success have no meaning."

—BENJAMIN FRANKLIN

You now possess the foundational knowledge of the characteristics needed for you to build your gypsy success securely. It is time for us to dive into the life skills you must practice daily in order to fully unleash your gypsy spirit. Give yourself a pat on the back and do a little dance, you are doing great! Need help with the dance part? Hop on my website and find some fun and easy dance moves that will help you.

Consider for a moment the cost you have paid physically, emotionally, and spiritually by living your life the same way you have year after year. What will your life look like if you do not harness these skills and make changes? Do you want your life to look exactly the same next year as it does today? If that brings you joy then great! If not, I encourage you to commit to changing. I know you have what it takes to

ANDREA B. RIGGS

implement these life-changing rituals because I know your desire to live an adventurous life is stirring inside of you.

To sum up what we've learned so far, GYPSY stands for:

1. **(G)ratitude** - for life and the abundance all around you.
2. **(Y)es** - to YOU!
3. **(P)ositive Purpose** - the intent in all you do.
4. **(S)elf-Love** - encompasses the limitless confidence you have within your soul for self-expression.
5. **(Y)oung at Heart** - because all gypsies love to play, dance, laugh, and enjoy life...even embracing the times they trip.

I want to take a moment to address how awesome life is. How delicious that we can do anything we want. We truly are creators, artists, and powerful organizers of energy. I love this aspect of life so you will see it sprinkled throughout my books such as my parenting book. Parenting is a fascinating topic to me. We have always been complemented on how we are raising our children and the people they are becoming. Choosing to parent intentionally, we spend a lot of time with our children. We believe we are meant to live intentional lives. What better gift can we give our children than the powerful ability to realize how instrumental their creative spirits are in designing the life they want?

When thinking about how to become a gypsy, you must be thoughtful and intentional. In order to unleash your family's gypsy spirit and live an adventurous life you must be willing to step out of the box and do things you are not used to doing.

This is your time and it all begins with you. I will outline all that you need within this workbook. I encourage you to move toward your purpose; it's the way we are built. Your next step is accountability. As that will ensure you get to where you want to go.

These life-changing tools will transform your world to the extent you are willing to commit to them. Finding your gypsy spirit takes time, persistence, determination, and as with anything, a certain amount of failures. Let's be honest, many of us lose focus after a few hours, sometimes even minutes. In order to change this, you must commit to what you are focused on attracting into your life, each day.

You will begin to set your priorities by using daily rituals. To make it easy for you, these rituals can be remembered through an acronym, WORTHY. This word helps remind you of the daily activities you must do in order to cultivate, grow, and realize all that you would like to become. They are lessons to remind you of your greatness and ways to connect to your highest good.

Worthy stands for the following:

- **W**isdom
- **O**ne Thing
- **R**eflection
- **T**rusting
- **H**ealth
- **Y**our True Value

You will learn to embrace the wisdom that these principles are founded upon. Once you have developed the skill sets I am offering, you will be able to create your life intentionally with your power from the highest form of consciousness. From there anything is possible and adventure becomes a natural extension of the life you choose to create.

A gypsy humbly remembers she is worthy of all things that are full of light and abundance including: wisdom, truth, goodness, success, and freedoms available. You, my dear gypsy, are worthy of all you want to create that is good. All the rest is just an old story so choose to let it go. These tips will help you do just that. Remember, this is not a one-time "letting go" event, but rather an on going journey that we are all in together.

I want to take a quick moment to thank you for your time and dedication. I know I am asking a lot of you, but I promise it is for your benefit and healing. My focus is to build you up through ways that I 100% believe in because I've seen them work again and again. When we become the powerful humans we are meant to become, we will align ourselves to create more magic within one community than has ever been done before. Welcome to the Gypsy Living Community. You are welcomed and wanted.

Now let's get started with recognizing that you are "worthy" of all you have ever wanted for your life.

Take an inventory of how you are feeling about yourself and your future. Are you learning anything new?

_____

_____

_____

_____

_____

_____

DOODLE PAGE

IX

"W" is for wisdom

*"Wisdom comes with the ability to be still.
Just look and just listen. No more is needed.
Being still, looking, and listening activates the
non-conceptual intelligence within you. Let
stillness direct your words and actions."*

—ECKHART TOLLE

Let's start by breaking down the attributes of WORTHY now beginning with wisdom. If you want to be well read, you read. If you want to be a good swimmer, you swim, a lot. If you want to master a concept, you teach it. If you want to be wise, you realize how insignificant, yet how significant you truly are. As Socrates tells us, "The only true wisdom is in knowing you know nothing." Wisdom is not taught—it is felt. Wisdom is not something you do—it is something you are. There is no finish line for wisdom, quite the opposite in fact. It is the realization that we are a small *and* very important piece of a much grander puzzle.

Wisdom connects you to the gypsy ancestors from the beginning of time. The love, blood, sweat, and the tears.

All of it. As you tap into your intuitive wisdom, you have the right to tap into your gypsy spirit ancestors' power from the beginning of time. This feminine life force energy is real. It is beyond the physical and connects us in a web-like structure, which far surpasses this human existence.

The universal truth that *is* your gypsy spirit is stitched together from many lives. You are not simply your own, but a culmination of thousands of people's DNA. You are in them and they are in you. Not only physically, but metaphysically as well. By tapping into your inner wisdom, you will begin to thirst for knowledge, truth, and understanding. From this place of awareness, true connection and trust emerges.

Think of the greatest minds of all time, and those you look up to. Think of our forefathers and the endless hours they spent cultivating wisdom through studying and introspection, watching nature, and interacting with others without technology. Wisdom is more than schooling and a degree; it is an internal awareness for truth and connection.

Wisdom encompasses personal development, which is an integral part of your continual thirst as a gypsy, for it is the preparation for life's coming events. Wisdom expands your curiosities, broadens your mind, teaches you compassion, and quite literally humbles you as you continue to understand on a deeper level. With learning comes understanding. With understanding comes compassion, clarity, and wisdom. It is the untamed mind that allows all that enters in to rule its world. What will rule your world? Wisdom I hope.

Gypsies are able to travel and explore because of the foundation on which they have built their values *and* because they know that each adventure is a chance to learn and discover something new about herself. You are gaining this skill and soon, you will allow yourself this new found joy in discovery.

Wisdom also encompasses reading, learning, and truly sinking our gypsy teeth into all we hunger to learn. For me, this includes reading, studying, writing and really sitting with information. It is important that we remain curious as we seek answers and understanding.

I learned an extremely useful tool I want to share with you that unlocks my wisdom and provides me with clarity. Upon rising, or anytime I have numerous thoughts running through my head, I pull out my journal and write continuously for five minutes or longer. Nothing matters during this time; it is just open space for wisdom to come through. As we commit to reading and/or writing each day and studying those mysteries that are most intriguing to us, the world and our own intuition will deepen and grow.

I recommend a minimum of 10 minutes a day, and up to an hour or more if you can make the time. Choose what works best for you. The key here is quality not quantity. Even if only one sentence strikes you to the core at that moment, embrace it, feel it, and continue to let your mind and journey expand.

<u>Action Exercise:</u>

(Choose one daily):

1. Continuous flow writing for 5 minutes, without a specific focus or point. This time will let the thoughts in your mind go, emptying your cup in order to make

room for more wisdom that really matters. *(I learned this from Jeffery T. Sooey, coach extraordinaire.)*

2. Read or listen to a book or topic of your choice for 20 minutes. From your session, compile the information into one sentence that was your "take-away." *(I learned this from Jeff Hoffman, co-author of SCALE Co-creator of Priceline.com, and my dear friend.)*

3. For 10-20 minutes look and listen to the world around you without saying anything. Notice what you take away from it. Do you listen on a deeper level? Do you usually interrupt because you have to be heard? What did you learn by being silent? *(Inspired by Eckhart Tolle)*

4. What do you want to understand about life on a deeper level? Research, find out, learn, experience, and look within. *(Inspired by my journey through life and my own cravings.)*

I believe we are our own greatest teacher. While I love being with people, especially my family, I realize that many of the times wisdom emerges in my life I am alone. Either on a hike or out in nature usually. Other times I am reading a book and pause to allow the words that struck me the chance to settle into the fibers of my being.

When I am seeking wisdom it is usually because I am struggling with something in my life. Even though I am open to wisdom entering my life, I believe I must be in the right state in order to embrace it. Wisdom is all around us. It is the embrace part and acceptance part that can brush up against our ego and create negative feelings. Wisdom takes compassion and a perspective that can see the entire journey, instead of the swamp that you are stuck in. Wisdom is gained through each decision and experience. And mostly wisdom is about the ever present truth that you are enough.

Which of these exercises intrigues you? Write about it now. What questions do you have about it that you can ask in our Facebook community?

_____

_____

_____

_____

_____

_____

_____

_____

_____

_____

_____

_____

_____

_____

_____

_____

_____

_____

_____

_____

_____

_____

_____

_____

_____

DOODLE PAGE

X

"O" is for one thing

"What is the ONE thing I can do such that by doing it everything else will be easier or unnecessary?"

—GARY KELLER, THE ONE THING

We store less information in our minds than in any other time in history. I am going to make a claim here that *many* of us struggle with distractions and an overactive mind, whether labeled ADD type behaviors or that we are simply challenged with disruptions. We live in the information age and we are surrounded by constant interruptions.

How many times do you sit at your computer to accomplish a specific task and end up on Facebook or some other social networking site? Before you know it, 15 minutes went by and you forgot what you were even going to do to begin with. In your spare moments, what are your go-to time wasters? We all know there are more meaningful things to do, however, the rush of the scroll (scrolling through websites) is habit-forming and our brains can easily become addicted to it.

The world outside can be similar to the *Strip* in Las Vegas with colors, lights, and sexy things begging for our attention. It's hard to deny or abstain from because most of us enjoy it. Why? Because it's fun, it's new, it's exciting, it's the next thing, and it's the latest and greatest! Our brain thinks, *hey this is important stuff and I'm getting a huge dopamine rush so let me stay in this euphoria just a little bit longer. It doesn't matter that I had a task that I was trying to focus on. Oh, hey, what was it anyway?*

I know you do this to a certain extent, because I do it too! Most likely, we will continue to struggle with this as long as technology makes our desires attainable with a click. The key to success is allowing yourself that time when it makes sense, and not allowing it to take over the precious time you have dedicated towards your "one thing." "O" represents the "one thing" in your life that you are working towards more than anything else.

There is a book fittingly called, *The One Thing* by Gary Keller. I highly recommend it. It clearly points out that when we continue to ask ourselves the question posed at the beginning of the chapter—*"What is the ONE thing I can do such that by doing it everything else will be easier or unnecessary?"*—we focus, create solutions, and actually get to where we want to go by doing only that which we are most closely aligned with.

Go deep and listen. You want something. You want something to change, grow, or to transform in your life. Be it a different lifestyle, career, relationship, financial gain, career success, love, or energy. What is it for you? What do you want? This is one of the most important questions you can ask yourself.

You have aspects of your life that are more important than others. You need to live, eat, maintain shelter, and have clothing. If you have a family, their needs are on the list too. You may feel pulled in a few different directions at times and this can be partly caused by saying "yes" to too many people and allowing distractions into your life.

There is no one to point your finger at because this is your own doing (as mean as it sounds). It's your ability or inability to stay focused on what you want that determines your success. If you want to see a change in your life and accomplish your "one thing," you must change the way you live your life so you can make room for it. It sounds simple, but first you must change the way you live your seconds, minutes, days, weeks, and months. To flip the coin and look at it from another perspective, what will it cost if you don't set out into the wild yonder to accomplish your "one thing?"

A gypsy knows what she wants. You must discover what you want in order to become a gypsy, so go for it!

Action Exercise:

1. Write down everything you do *not* want.

    _____
    _____
    _____
    _____
    _____

2. Write down the opposite of everything you don't want and focus on what you DO want.

    _____
    _____

_____

_____

_____

3. Take your pen and scribble or cross out the list of things you *don't* want.

4. Using the list of things you *do* want, write down 5 things that you could do in order to obtain what you DO want.

   1. _____
   2. _____
   3. _____
   4. _____
   5. _____

5. Look at the list, what feels good? Why?

_____

_____

_____

_____

_____

6. What is the one thing you can do in order to obtain what you want? Trust yourself; you have the answers inside of you. If you are unsure, this is why our community and guides are here. You are supported.

_____

_____

_____

_____

_____

What you want is simple when you lose the hype surrounding everything except the one thing you would like to accomplish. Your "one thing" may be a skill you want to develop like playing the flute or dancing beautifully in pointe shoes, like my daughter Lucy. It may be to go on an adventure or acquire financial success (whatever that means to you). No matter what your "one thing" is, you must be able to define what it is and commit to it, making the necessary adjustments along the way. Institute playfulness here. It is okay not to have all the answers. Picking your "one thing" this week may lead you to another "one thing" the week after, and that is the beauty of adventure. Each time you will get closer and closer to what it is that you really want.

So what is it that you want? Are you ready to see it, feel it, and taste it?

That comes next. Below write about your feelings about your "one thing." What does your head say and what does your heart say? Can you align them both?

_____

_____

_____

_____

_____

_____

_____

_____

_____

_____

_____

_____

_____

DOODLE PAGE

XI

"R" is for reflection

"If you want to awaken all of humanity, then awaken all of yourself. If you want to eliminate the suffering in the world, then eliminate all that is dark and negative in yourself. Truly, the greatest gift you have to give is that of your own self-transformation."

—LAO TZU

"R" is for reflection, and if you let it, the powerful information in this chapter can transform your world. Within reflection lies the key to opening up your entire gypsy world. As stated previously, a gypsy can sit still with herself, while using her breath to separate from her mind so she can take the seat of her consciousness. This concept may be new, it was for me when I first heard it, yet I was so intrigued! Let's break it down.

Self-reflection helps you learn about your true self by putting you in touch with the master of your ship, you. When you close your mouth and turn your attention inward, you begin to notice the inner turmoil and constant noise and chatter that has become a part of your thought process and action patterns. As you breathe, create space, and focus on your inner world, you begin the process of healing by finding consciousness at the deepest introspective level. When tapped into, you can even begin to clearly hear and feel your own inner gypsy spirit. Your intuition protects your gypsy spirit and since you were born with it, it can never be lost. So, do not lose heart if you are not in touch with yours, it is there and through reflection, you will become one with your inner voice.

Before we go any further, it is important to recognize the physical aspect of this concept. Your pineal gland is located in the center of your brain. It's where your consciousness and intuition physically take place. You have an actual body part dedicated to your intuition, isn't that so amazing?! This is real my friend, and you are entitled to merge with your magnificent intuition which is your highest frequency.

Your pineal gland is not the only body part that helps you out in this way. Your entire body wants to feel more peace, experience joy, and find meaning. Yet it has become increasingly difficult to tap into our ability because of the tremendous distractions and addictions to technology. If this topic intrigues you as much as it did me, I recommend a book called, *The Shallows* by Nicholas Carr. He shares that our brains are quite literally "adapting" and not in a good way.

In order to cultivate our gypsy spirit, we must be willing to live outside the norm, learning to detach from the world, others, and even our human experience every so often. Deepak Chopra teaches us "In stillness we find our true self." I want you to begin to see yourself differently— as an ultra-human or a spiritual being having a human experience. Connect yourself to an energy force that you feel strongly about. For me, Mother Earth—the feminine power and creative genius—is extremely powerful. Prana, for example, means breath or life force. This is also powerful for me. God or the Universe, it all works so choose what resonates for you!

It is now time to see yourself as you really are—perfectly imperfect, the creator of your universe, your life, and your moments. For it is in this space of ultimate creativity that your connection to a greater cause connects you and me. One of my favorite books about imperfection (which I have embraced through my yoga practice) is titled, *Perfectly Imperfect: The Art and Soul of Yoga Practice* by Baron Baptiste.

Reflection can take different forms each day, as you create a routine that serves you best during this period in your life. I encourage you to do what works, while it's working. In addition, remember when you lack focus, inspiration, or desire to realize it is time to switch gears and get playful with your reflection practice.

By shedding the layers of your superficial images, even your ego, you will begin to consciously tether yourself to that higher power. By doing so, your world and point of view will begin to change for good. You will allow what "must" be in your life to fall away to allow for all that "can" and "will" become in your life.

As you prepare for your own reflection practice, think about combining the exercise in a way that feels good to you. One option is to break down 15 minutes of reflection into something like this:

1. 5 minutes of clearing the mind/stillness
2. 5 minutes of affirmations
3. 5 minutes of visualizations

You can access a free 15-minute sample session at www. GypsyFam.com/GypsyLivingTips.

Action Exercises:

1. Clearing the Mind (Mindfulness/Meditation)

First, clear your mind by letting thoughts drift through and out of your head like balloons. I imagine my thoughts are red balloons. I see them come and then float gently out of my mind, up, up and away. Begin to notice your body, your bones, your joints, and your heartbeat.

Some tips to help with clearing your mind:

a. Sit by the ocean or in nature and notice your surroundings. Let your mind be open and curious about all the wonder around you.

b. Listen to meditative music and simply notice your breathing and the sensations in your body.

c. Use the resources I provide online at www.GypsyFam. com/GypsyLivingTips as guidance, or anything that works for you.

2. Affirmations

Next, affirm the wonderful human you already are by choosing to connect with your gypsy spirit through affirmations. Affirmations are verbal manifestations of what you want to create, as well as, power statements and questions to assist you in finding your own solutions.

a. You can come up with your own.

b. It is wise to form the affirmation with a "why" question instead of a statement. For example, instead of saying, "I am Worthy!" ask, "Why am I worthy?" This gives your mind the opportunity to contemplate yourself in a positive light. Over time, you will create new neuro pathways in the brain by practicing these exercises consistently. The brain will absolutely hop on board with these new measures to unleash your gypsy spirit, however, it's important to stay positive, focused, and consistent. Stay the course and do not give up. When you ask questions such as, "Why am I so amazing?" The brain is forced to come up with a solution, such as, "because I am inherently full of light and truth" and you will literally begin thinking about yourself in a positive light.

c. You can think them, yell them, and look at yourself in the mirror while you say them, whatever works for you. Choose a form that is empowering to you.

d. There is no right or wrong way. The focus is on teaching our brains—both the subconscious and conscious minds—to think positively about ourselves and to realize what matters and what does not. We are creating space within.

e. Be creative and intentional about who and what you want to create. Make this meaningful. Going through the motions is not enough, you must be present, and express with your feelings because everything begins from our emotions.

Can you commit to this? _____

Why? _____

_____

_____

_____

How will you do it?

_____

_____

_____

Where will you do it?

_____

_____

_____

3. Visualizations

Finally, you will learn how to powerfully visualize and manifest what you want through your mind's eye into your future through visualization.

1. Eyes can be open or closed, although I recommend closed.

2. Begin to imagine and to create pictures of what you want in your future.

3. Gather people you love around you in your visualizations as often as you need in order to feel

supported, loved, and encouraged to go where you want to go.

4. Imagine your future and create your life's movie. Smile, breathe, cry, and be one with your dream. Let that fill every cell of your body.

5. No one is judging you so let yourself feel free while doing this. There is no expectation, judgement, or competition. Let go of feeling silly and realize that this powerful tool bridges the gap between where you *are* and where you *want* to be.

What feelings come up for you about this concept?

_____

_____

_____

_____

_____

_____

_____

_____

_____

_____

My dear gypsy, soon you will begin to do these practices automatically. You can practice them at different times of the day—in your car waiting for a light to change to green, with your kids, at the beach, even waiting for an appointment. This is the true gift of harnessing this seat of consciousness and its ability to help you look at your life, and even another's, through a different perspective. This alternative viewpoint gives us reason to pause.

I learned this wonderful tool from yoga instructor and mentor, Hala Khouri, that I adapted for myself.

Action Exercise:

1. **Notice.** what is going on around you in your busy life. Separate yourself from the emotion or reaction that is typically your "normal" response.

2. **Ground.** It is important to ground yourself. This allows us you to think about who you are and how you want to be, act, and live. What do you want to create? What and who supports you?

3. **Center yourself.** Look within and notice that you have a choice of whether to react or to respond. It is important that you try taking the seat of consciousness here.

4. **Take a deep breath and move with your intuition.** Drishti is breath. As you focus on your breath, you will notice that it pulls your focus. The more you focus on your breath, the sooner you will see how you can learn to focus on one thing.

I have been a student of yoga since junior high. I gravitated towards it from the first moment I was introduced to it by my friend's mother in her sun-filled kitchen with the yellow parakeet chirping in the background. All of us school girls laughed at the names of the poses like, "down dog." I believe we naturally go towards that which moves us, and since I was a teenager, yoga has drawn me in and I have continually moved towards it.

This entire chapter is part of my rehabilitative yoga practice. I whole-heartedly encourage you to do the same in your yoga practice or the physical exercise of your choice. I believe doing so adds extra benefits, both seen and unseen. During moving meditation, our body flows to internal and external rhythms that increase blood flow and mental and physical stimulation, elevating and intensifying reflection.

I teach Baptiste inspired yoga and many forms of fitness in addition to my own personal practice. I have learned that I can take what I practice on my mat, and utilize it off the mat as well. My life has become a moving yoga practice, and in many ways, a moving meditation as well. I encourage you to seek out a Baptiste Yoga Studio if there is one in your area, and try a Power Yoga class. If not, any yoga class that suits your needs at this time is a great choice. It is my belief that as you align your body, mind, and spirit through this age-old practice, you will become more in touch with your gypsy spirit each day.

Reflection is the practice of you becoming aware of you. This is a practice which none of us will ever master. It is the space created within your world for clarity. Doing yoga and meditating once a day will help you. Learning to be aware, to ground, to center, and to breathe will help you. Realize that nothing lasts forever. For years, I did yoga to simply make it through the day. Reflection is not meant to be a coping mechanism. It is an art, not a science. Art is messy and you tend to get dirty. My intention as you leave this chapter is simple. *I want you to know that reflection allows you to uncover the layers of distrust in yourself and others. It sheds the layers of hurt and opens you up to your greatness not on an annual basis, but a daily basis.* One day, who knows, you may even begin to learn the art of moment-by-moment reflections. Something for us all to work towards, which is why it is a practice.

Keep this in mind. With each exhale, you let go of negativity and that which does not serve you. In addition, with each inhale you fill your horizon with approval, compassion, and worthiness of all you want to create. I honor your journey.

What will you take away from this chapter?

_____
_____
_____
_____
_____
_____
_____
_____
_____
_____

How will you implement this into your life?

_____
_____
_____
_____
_____
_____
_____
_____
_____
_____

What "Ah-ha" moments did you have?

_____

_____

_____

_____

_____

_____

_____

_____

_____

_____

DOODLE PAGE

XII

"T" is for trusting

"Trust the Universe. Trust and believe and have faith. I truly had no idea how I was going to bring the knowledge of The Secret onto the movie screen. I just held to the outcome of the vision, I saw the outcome clearly in my mind, I felt it with all my might, and everything that we needed to create The Secret came to us."

—RHONDA BYRNE

There are two types of people in this world—those who trust life and those who do not. To trust life is to trust *in* life, meaning you know without a doubt that she is going to show up for you, take care of you, and continually hold you gently in her hand. There is nothing you can or cannot do to change the fact that you are loved and will be taken care of. Nothing.

To trust life is to believe in something larger than yourself, whether you call it God, The Universe, Mother Earth, Prana, or anything full of light and energy that works for you. Sometimes we confuse faith with religion, and spirituality with people who attend church. I take an opposite and more spiritually grounded approach. You do not have to be religious to be spiritual. Spirituality is simple and it is beautiful. It connects you to me and both of us to a larger universal power. What do you believe in?

Action Exercise:

- Where does your higher power belief stem from?

  _____
  _____
  _____
  _____
  _____

- Have you ever considered not believing in this form of power?

  _____
  _____
  _____
  _____
  _____

- Have you ever lived without trusting in a universal power or energy force?

  _____
  _____
  _____
  _____
  _____

- If so, what was that experience like?

  _____
  _____

_____

_____

_____

- What do *you* believe in?

_____

_____

_____

_____

- Why do you believe in that source of power?

_____

_____

_____

_____

- What would your future look like if you were to upgrade your trust in a life force that included all of these qualities:
  o   No judgement
  o   No competition
  o   No expectation
  o   Unconditional love
  o   Assurance you would be taken care of
  o   A strong tethered connection
  o   Full of light and truth

_____

_____

_____

_____

_____

- What would it take for you to let go of the way you have seen your paradigm, religion, or belief system and to learn to include these qualities for you and everyone you interact with?

  _____

  _____

  _____

  _____

  _____

- What would it take for you to see that you cannot control the outcome of your life or anyone else's?

  _____

  _____

  _____

  _____

  _____

- What would it take for you to let go of control and allow the Universe to take care of you?

  _____

  _____

  _____

  _____

  _____

- What would it take for you to trust in THIS kind of power and energy source?

  _____

  _____

  _____

  _____

  _____

Trust is a two-way relationship. As such, you must believe in something larger than yourself, even if it is simply an organizing power. For me, even as a child, I have always felt that the female energy of the earth is incredibly strong. At the same time, I was raised to believe in God and Jesus Christ. As I grew up and increased my yoga practice, my own beliefs began to emerge. It took me well into my thirties to vocalize what *I* truly believed, not what I was told I should believe. This came after years of research, curiosity, learning, introspection, and meditation. My journey fostered a great deal of respect for my own path as well as the individual journey of others.

Action Exercise:

• What do you know beyond a shadow of a doubt?

_____

_____

_____

_____

_____

• Have you questioned that?

_____

_____

_____

_____

• Question it and consider that what you believe is not true.

_____

_____

_____

_____

_____

- How do you feel? It is only through questioning and considering that you will uncover the truth about your relationship with life and the trust you have.

_____

_____

_____

_____

_____

- What would it take for you to let go of any ill feelings or guilt that you have surrounding trusting the flow of life?

_____

_____

_____

_____

_____

- What is the consequence if you do *not* do this?

_____

_____

_____

_____

_____

- What effect will it have on you to continue living life without trust?

_____

_____

_____

_____

_____

- What would it take for you to trust in life?

_____

_____

_____

_____

_____

I get it. In this day and age, we want to be better, faster, quicker, and richer. We want to hard-nose our way to success and prosperity. We want the ticket that will get us straight to the top. We rev our engines and hit the tracks running. We own our destiny!

We can build our own websites, create our own businesses, and become an overnight success (although "overnight" usually takes 10 years). Allow me to point out that typically, this is a life filled with stress because you have a tight grip on the outcome. Speaking from first-hand experience here, the problem with this approach is that you lead with your head instead of your heart. When you have feelings come up, you learn to stamp them out or stuff them deep inside.

While you may take time for a five-minute mediation or do "some" introspection work during the day, this is typically not enough. Why? You make thousands of decisions daily and with each comes an emotion and feeling. This is magic. How you feel matters and your gypsy spirit (your inner voice and intuition) is the best guide you have. You must learn to trust in that. You must learn to trust her as your guide, confident that this is how the Universe speaks to you.

It is a good idea to get comfortable with the fact that you don't always have control over some of the events that you encounter in life. However, you *do* create your world and you have more control over the outcome during meditation than you ever dreamed possible. Through visualizing, feeling, and setting your intentions, the Universe responds. It may not be the path that you chose, nor the way you thought your dream would happen, but happen it will. As you throw your dreams out into the Universe like glitter, you allow your desires to find a way to root. As your dreams root in the Universe, little by little you will begin to see your life change. The more you trust, the more you will see that you can do a lot less yet accomplish much more. Intention has massive universal organizing power.

My husband hates glitter. My kids and I love it! Every time he sees the bottle of glitter come out, his eyes grow five times as large and his gasps of horror echo through the air. When I see his reaction to the glitter, I laugh. He still hates glitter, I think, because it is sticky, gets everywhere, and is impossible to clean up. We find it in his beard, on his back, maybe on an eyelid, in the food, and on the kitchen scrub brush. It is just so sticky!

This is a good way to think about your dream, your glitter, and your ability to trust. As you send out your sticky glitter dreams into the Universe, they will stick where they need to go. Just like the glitter found in Charles' beard, we do not choose where the glitter goes. It will find its home all on its own. That is the trust you can now adopt—simply by putting out what you want, your dreams will come back to you tenfold. People will show up to support you and your desires. The only catch—you must believe 100%.

You have the ability to move people and energy forces simply by using your intention. An intention is a strong desire of consciousness for your life. Some believe it is like a prayer. Although to your rational mind it may seem ironic, life is this way and your gypsy spirit will tell you so. The key is to understand that in this connection you play a key role—a creator. You and the energy of your choosing—God, the Universe, Prana, Mother Nature—co-create together. Whatever you can dream can be. Remember, the way you internalize your dreams and trust the beauty of life to unfold, matters.

The older I get the more clearly I can see those that live by this code and those who do not. Trusting in life stems from our first chakra and the need to belong. Think about someone you trust. Hold their image in your mind's eye. Now think about someone who you do *not* trust. Why don't you trust them?

_____

_____

_____

_____

_____

_____

_____

_____

_____

For years, I have been coaching (I prefer the term guided as stated previously) clients in fitness, life challenges, nutrition, healing the gut, and disempowering beliefs. I have found that the main reason people fail is because of their lack of trust. More specifically, a lack of trust in the flow of life.

Usually this is because on a very deep internal level that trust was violated and they learned to be cautious and live defensively. The inherent trust of a child is a magical trait, but sadly, few keep it. Whether by neglect, abuse, or a decision made by the child, the trust they once had gets lost. Later in life, this can show up in many ways—poor relationships, unfulfilling careers, depression, and all types of diseases.

Trusting in life is an extremely important part of embracing your gypsy spirit. If you don't already, I know that you can learn to trust life. This can be a gentle and compassionate process.

Action Exercise:

• What do you fear?

_____

_____

_____

_____

_____

• What is holding you back from living the life you want?

_____

_____

_____

_____

_____

• In what areas of your life do you feel you must MAKE IT HAPPEN?

_____

_____

_____

_____

_____

• In what areas could you trust more?

_____

_____

_____

_____

• Can you let go of the past to create space for the future?

_____

_____

_____

_____

• How can you do this?

_____

_____

_____

_____

• Do you recall a past event that you need to face where your trust was betrayed?

_____

_____

_____

_____

- If so, take responsibility today to mend it, for you and for them. Text, call, or compassionately confront them.

  _____

  _____

  _____

- Did you do it?

  _____

  _____

  _____

- How did it go?

  _____

  _____

  _____

- Humans are humans. As such, we are all imperfect. Are you able to let others walk their path, as you walk and take responsibility for yours and yours alone?

  _____

  _____

  _____

  _____

  _____

- In which areas of your life can you trust the flow of life to take care of you?

  _____

  _____

  _____

  _____

  _____

As you begin to move through this journey, you will slowly begin to see that as stated above, there are two kinds of people on earth—those who trust life and those who do not.

<u>Action Exercise:</u>

- Write down three people you know, who trust life.
   1. _____
   2. _____
   3. _____

- Write down three people, you know, who do *not* trust life.
   1. _____
   2. _____
   3. _____

- What is the difference between the two groups?

   _____

   _____

   _____

- Why do you think it is easy for those who trust in life to be happy?

   _____

   _____

   _____

- What is the one thing you can do on a daily basis to develop more trust in the Universe to take care of you?
   1. _____
   2. _____
   3. _____

By learning to trust life once again, you can begin to live with childlike wonder and curiosity. If you do not believe in anything right now and you feel alone, I am here to tell you that you are *not* alone. You are deeply connected to more than you could ever comprehend in your mind. You were connected to the energy of the Universe long before you were born, and you will continue to belong after you *physically* die. You are connected to people, creatures, and everything through energy.

You do not have to believe in a glowing white God who sits in heaven, nor do you have to believe that in order to get into heaven you must fit through the Buddha's nostril. You do not have to believe in anything other than what you feel inside. Discover what is true for you and stay curious.

<u>Action Exercise:</u>

* What do you feel is true inside for you?

\
\
\
\
\

* Do you have a relationship with that energy force?

\
\
\
\
\

- How do you communicate with that energy force?

  _____

  _____

  _____

  _____

  _____

- Take a moment and write for 5 minutes continuously about what you trust in. Write down your questions, what you *want* to trust in, and how your life is changing because you are learning to trust in life once again.

_____

_____

_____

_____

_____

_____

_____

_____

_____

_____

_____

_____

_____

_____

_____

_____

_____

_____

_____

_____

_____

The deeper you trust in life, the more resilient you will become. Let me repeat that so you really take it in. The deeper you trust (the flow of) life, the more resilient you will become. What does this mean? The more you can appreciate the peaks *and* the valleys, the more capable you'll become at handling challenges *and* the easier it will be for you to roll with the punches. The deeper your trust in the Universe and your creative expression that flows from it, the easier life's up's and down's become.

This is where the essence of your gypsy spirit comes from. As you begin to live truly from your heart, believing that life will show up for you 100%, your life will become easier. You now have the choice to believe that life will always give you exactly what you need. It won't matter anymore whether your journey takes a different path or the outcome changes, you will know that you will always be looked out for. Your sparkles and dreams are already out there in the universe so all that you have to do is stay focused on what you want and know that if your path gets derailed, it is for a good reason that is for your highest benefit.

Remember, if your plan is not working out, let go, and breathe. If you feel frustration, remember it is because you are wanting to control the path. Don't worry, something better is right around the corner. Do not hope, but know this with 100% conviction. You are the creator, so create what you want. Ask yourself the questions, and let your mind offer solutions. I expanded upon this in the previous chapter and laid the groundwork so you can now see how reflection plays into trust.

There is an undeniable link between reflection and trusting. It is through reflection that you exercise your ability to trust.

It is through this trust that doing the work will make a difference in your life. If you do not fully believe reflection will enhance your life, you will not put everything you have into it. Even if you do believe it will change your life, actually doing it is quite another thing. This requires you learning and embracing the way it works for you.

Let's say you are a mom who has responsibilities to your children on top of working outside of the home. This may make you feel that you do *not* have time for consistent meditation. A concept that I have learned which has allowed me to overcome this is understanding that I can meditate anytime and anywhere. Whether I'm sitting in my living room with commotion all around me, driving by the ocean and appreciating it for a mere five seconds as I whiz by, or breathing my way into a meditative state wherever I am.

Trust in yourself that you can learn these concepts and gently allow them to blend into your life like a beautiful tie-dyed shirt. No worries, mine is going to look different from yours, so there is no expectation. You are given the space here to explore and see where your trust lies. Explore it. See what works for you and that which does not, and make the changes necessary to elevate you, your mind, and your state of being.

The people you see living life to the fullest with an open heart, trust life. You can too. You can take responsibility right now for the lack of trust that you may have had until this point. With your mind's eye, you can do all the work you must in order to unleash your gypsy spirit. You deserve to live your best life full of trust. So trust. Do *not* focus on being burned or taken advantage of. Trust that you will be loved and supported no matter what. Whatever it is you seek, you find, so seek abundance.

The last exercise is one that you can practice on a daily basis to increase your trusting muscle in the life force you believe in. This is an exercise that is to be done as soon as you experience dis-trust and dis-ease in your life. The more frequent you do it AS SOON as a challenge arises, the quicker you will learn to shift your focus from dis-trust to trust. Simply follow this three-step rule when you feel yourself giving weight to problems, challenges, and hardships in your life.

Action Exercise:

1. Take a deep breath and look up.
2. As you look up, imagine many angels (or energies) that are there waiting for you to give them a command.
3. Give them the command. Ask them to take care of all you want. As you find the solutions in your mind, send them to take care of all you need. If you cannot find solutions, ask simply for the solutions to be poured into your mind, or a new avenue opened up to you. Soon you will learn to trust.

Life does not give you what you want; it gives us something much better. When you stay open and create space for it, the goodness will come from every direction.

Trust in life. Trust in others. Look for life to support you in all you do. Shift your thinking to this way and your life will change 180 degrees more quickly than you imagine. Aligning with your intuition will give you the necessary trust in yourself from source to live your greatest adventure. Little by little, day by day, your gypsy spirit will continue to open from this deep connected place. This is an unseen place, but you will feel the connection and trust from the network that you are now a part of. As you trust in this deep connected synergy, you will feel better than you have ever felt in your life, fully understanding your value and worth. You will finally see what I see—that you are incredible and life has so much joy in store for you!

DOODLE PAGE

XIII

"H" is for health

"To elevate the body is to elevate the mind, to elevate the mind is to elevate the spirit. True health encompasses this trifecta. Anytime we discount one there is a deficit made in our life. Health is about learning about you, your body, and what makes you tic. Health is about learning to enjoy the journey and staying curious about how you internalize your world. Health is the key to life, in turn, life is the key to your health. Armed with the time tested truths of the ages, you alone have the power to turn the key."

—ANDREA B. RIGGS

I've come to understand that health is sacred. The art of healing has been a life long struggle, journey, and eventually a success for me. If health was something we all had 100% control over, we would all be living, but we are not. Steve Jobs had plenty of zero's in his bank account to cover any lifesaving medical procedures, yet we know he is no longer with us physically. This brings up questions such as—can we even control our health? What can we do? How and why are "healthy" people dying?

The entire health industry in America is convoluted, yet, good health is *the* most important aspect of our humanity. Health has a different meaning to each of us, for obvious reasons. Both you and I can use the word and say, "I am eating super healthy these days." Yet, there is no foundation from which to pull from that is encompassed by all. Why?

This is due to the fact that we are all on our own journey and have different perspectives and experiences. We pull information from varied sources and internalize this into our subconscious mind. Ironically, it seems that the mass amount of information at our fingertips has not helped much. In most cases, it hasn't helped at all. If you research statistics about mental health diseases alone, you will see that. Look into obesity and overweight stats in America and you will find major problems. Concerning food and diet, anything is acceptable. You can find someone whose beliefs back your habits. Naturally, whatever we seek, we find. Most likely, you have a belief system surrounding health and I want you to know that I honor your journey and your path, even your truth. Mostly, I am grateful for the choice you made which brought us together here and now, so that I can share what true health means to me through my experiences, research, and curiosity, as well as, my struggles and joy.

Know that nothing I write in this book is true or false. These words are a compilation of my experiences, knowledge, and energy. Some concepts will ring true for you, and others may seem odd, either way, thank you for being open and listening. I am grateful for the ability to continuously learn, grow, and challenge myself. Were I not a truth seeker, this book would never have been written. To that end, may I welcome you to a place that is worth more than gold to me, health.

Most of us have gone through a trauma or health crisis, so I'm going to assume that you have dealt with some type of identity crisis, abuse, self-doubt, eating disorder of some nature, or self-medicating in one form or another, including addictions to caffeine, prescription pills, or drugs in any form. Maybe for you it was using exercise or over-eating as a way of escaping or controlling. Even optimism can be a form of "coping." From this perspective, do we not all have a similar struggle with health? And isn't that struggle, more often than not, an internal one?

All health begins with a very basic truth about how you feel about yourself. How do you learn the art of connecting to your health? How can you more fully be in tune with your body and your health? In this chapter, I will break down the pillars of gypsy health and lay a foundation from which you will be able to build your deep and lasting health.

I believe you are prepared for the information I'm about to share. Awareness is a powerful key to embracing the gypsy life. For a moment, put your current beliefs to the side to create space for something that I believe can change your life. I ask you to keep this important awareness at the forefront of your mind—*you are fully capable of learning to listen to your own intuition and body.*

From this place of power, we acknowledge that listening to the body takes time, stillness, peace, and focus. If you listen, your body is communicating with you all the time. For example, it lets you know when you are in pain, hungry, tired, thirsty, sad, or happy. The way you feel, internalize, and interpret your body's signals such as cognitive dissonance, internal turmoil and stress, matters.

If you live with a lack of ease in the way you internalize your world, this can be termed dis-ease in the body. Any dis-ease becomes disease as Louise Hay tells us in her book, *You Can Heal Your Life*. She explains that healing your life begins with changing the way you internalize life.

Feelings buried inside never die, and have so much more to do with your health than you may realize. Those negative feelings settle in and become knots of disempowering beliefs. Regret and remorse restrain the gypsy spirit, causing turmoil inside. These feelings lead to a disempowering life, and since our goal is the opposite of this, we must learn to utilize empowering tools that can unleash our gypsy spirits.

You will never arrive "at" health, as it is not a destination. Therefore, you must never be complacent in regards to it, for your body is complex, adaptive, and changes through many stages as it ages.

Your body is your vessel; how will you steer it? What will you venture into your adventure with? What adventures will you go on with this vessel? Will it be leaky in the middle of the ocean and sink? Will it ride through any storm because you know how to steer it? No one knows your body better than you do so don't believe that any expert can tell you what you need. You have been given a mind of your own; it is time for you to use it to serve yourself and your health by taking you in the direction *you* want to go.

The most introspective health paradigm for me is that of body, mind, and spirit. Millions have adopted this more conscious and interconnected view of health. You can intentionally let go of the separateness of the body, mind, and spirit and begin seeing them braided together.

Let's go into more detail. You have a physical body that houses your mind and spirit. This physical form is directly affected by the way you interpret your world *through* your mind and spirit. The way you see and feel is manifested into this form you call the body.

Inside of your body, you have a governing tool called your mind. This mind is a simulator for you and it never stops. It is the ongoing safety feature *and* the dream's ability to take action. It is the *how* to your spirit's *why*. When it follows the spirit, the mind can take you places you've only dreamed of.

You have a spirit, which I like to call your gypsy spirit. This spirit houses your purest intentions. It is the birthplace of adventure and dreams, and the true essence of who you really are. Your spirit—pure, clean and full of light—encompasses your heart, love, deepest desires, intentions, and the best of you. This spirit drives you in all you do. Without this, you would be just like everyone else on earth. Your gypsy spirit encompasses all of your perfections, imperfections, and all that makes you, you.

The body, mind, and spirit are meant to work in beautiful harmony. As the spirit leads the mind, and the mind leads the body, one is able to create a synergistic union of this trifecta. Each is able to see the deep connection one has with the other. When in harmony, they flow into and out of one another seamlessly.

Unfortunately, many people don't think about health in this manner. Instead they focus on calories in and calories out being the name of the game. Or they think, *let's get this workout in and sink our teeth into the next fad diet,* and so forth. These aspects of our health—movement and food choices—are extremely important, however, it's best to view them as a part of the whole cycle.

As we dive deeper into these topics, contemplate how food and movement nourish each area of the body, mind, and spirit. Food is the energy that nourishes the trifecta. The movement of the body infuses the trifecta with each inhale, exhale, and step taken. You can think of movement and nourishment as gifts that allow your body, mind, and spirit to give you their best in each moment of every day.

As you go through this chapter, my intention is for you to see that true health is more than following a diet book. It goes much deeper than the waistline. Health is a journey for each of us, so I ask that you have compassion for yours.

A little background—the fitness industry has been my playground and a top priority in my life for over a decade. Through instructing countless fitness classes in a variety of formats, I have worked out with thousands of people around the world. As a business owner, format creator, choreographer, contracted fitness professional, and a conference motivational movement expert, I've had the opportunity to affect countless lives. What you may not know is that these men and women have made a profound impact on my life as well. As I served, taught, and learned, I developed a deeper connection to others as well as myself. This is what helped me to discover what true healing means to me.

As an instructor, coach, and personal trainer, obtaining credentials drove me initially. I became a fitness and nutrition expert, held many Zumba ™ fitness certificates—ACE and AFAA—CPT with NASM, contracted fitness professional and began to dabble in my own fitness creations. Eventually I found my energy gravitating me towards becoming a Baptiste Certified Instructor and holding my own trainings.

As my journey continued, my desire to learn even more deepened. I became increasingly aware of the importance of true health especially when I saw clients fail. Each person that I helped—through every pound that was lost or gained, struggle, divorce, marriage, and dream that was built and torn down—peaked my need to develop further understanding. Why do people fail when it comes to health?

As fitness bled into nutrition and the importance of it, I began to learn more about supplementation and the body's deficits. Yes, unfortunately, our soils are depleted and most of our food is not nutritionally dense, so I recognized the need to make food "healthy" again. Through the discovery of fermentation and healing the gut, I felt the connectedness at the core of all health.

This eventually led me to discovering the essence of energy work, and combining it with healing the gut, and rehabilitative movement to create a paradigm that awakened within my gypsy spirit. As I embraced this truth, I realized this was the foundation of the gypsy spirit. Not just for me, but for all of us. The more I embraced my journey and taught others this information, the more I realized that people were ready for this.

Years ago, I believed that no one knew the truth and for a while, I lived within that mind frame. Over the past two years, I've felt an energy shift, (which was also mine of course) and I realized that this was no longer true. People are not only ready, but also hungry for this information. If you have any doubt, *you* are ready for it!

The dilemma that man has suffered from need, no longer must be. The awakenings that come as we connect through food and movement is undeniable. It all stems from energy. From my yoga class to the sauerkraut we make by hand, everything we do—each bite of food, back rub given or received, kiss goodbye, or smile—is a transfer of energy. All health is energy.

Let's take note of what true health means and looks like for you. Complete the following questions:

Action Exercise:

1. Write down what true health means to you.

_____

_____

_____

_____

_____

2. What does a life with true health look like for you?

_____

_____

_____

_____

_____

The best way to begin is to take the first step. The journey of health is ongoing so remember there is no finish line to claim or time period to end so we can go back to "normal." I invite you now to stay open, be ready, be a "yes" for you, and give up old ways of thinking and living that no longer serve you as we begin laying the foundation of your true health.

Your body is beautiful and that beauty begins on the inside. In order to have the gypsy exterior beauty, we must concentrate on the internal beauty first. The body, mind, and spirit are connected, and as such, we must dedicate time to caring for our body in order to have a healthy mind and spirit. A gypsy cannot have one out of alignment, so she is aware when there is an imbalance between these.

The Body

Caring for the physical manifestation of our gypsy spirit and mind.

1. Water is life. Drink as much mineral-rich natural spring water as humanely possible. It is important that it has not been treated with fluoride and other processes and procedures. You can get tips on how to test your water at www.GypsyFam.com/GypsyLivingTips.

2. Sleep is extremely important. Sleep 6-8 hours each night and when you are tired, rest. If you need naps, I recommend no longer than a 20-minute power nap. Listen to your body; you may need more rest than you think.

3. Ingredients to *always* avoid:
    a. High Fructose Corn Syrup (and sugar in general)
    b. GMO products
    c. Hydrogenated fats (including partially hydro-genated oils)
    d. Vegetable oils such as Canola
    e. Synthetic dyes (found in a significant amount of children's food, drinks, etc.)
    f. Store bought pasteurized dairy products (especially milk)
    g. Gluten and enriched wheat flour

4. Raw cow and goat milk of any kind is natural and nourishing. As long as it is purchased from a clean, safe source, you will be doing what people have been doing for thousands of years. Most dairy is highly processed and lacks the necessary enzymes to digest it properly.

5. Eat fermented foods and heal your gut (up to 40% of your diet).

6. Bone broth is key in restoring gut health (even for vegans). If I could suggest only one item to add to your diet, it would be bone broth. It heals the gut.

7. Eat nutritionally dense foods and buy from local growers (or grow your own) as much as possible.

8. Eat meat that is grass-fed and grass-finished without the use of GMO corn. (For more information visit my friends at www.Bar10Beef.com

9. Eliminate soda pop, juice, and sugary drinks and replace with water kefir and kombucha, and natural teas. (see www.ferementationforlife.com to learn more.)

10. Drink alcohol and coffee sparingly or consciously for special occasions only. The repetitive use of any of these can be habit forming.

What stands out for you from this list?

_____
_____
_____
_____
_____
_____
_____
_____
_____
_____
_____

What are you already doing?

_____
_____
_____
_____
_____
_____
_____
_____
_____
_____

What do you need help with?

_____

_____

_____

_____

_____

_____

_____

_____

_____

_____

What items do you have questions about?

_____

_____

_____

_____

_____

_____

_____

_____

_____

Much of the mainstream food in our culture causes an inflammatory response in our bodies, hence all the digestive issues and disease. By adopting the list above, you will dramatically decrease disease and inflammation. For some of you that may have sounded like a foreign language. Put another way, our body is meant to work; it is a machine. Just like a car, you can give it different types of fuel. The better the fuel, the better the machine will run. As you add impurities and even water down the fuel, the machine will not run quite as efficiently. Over time, this leaves the body with major deficits. The body is built to heal itself, so it does its best to carry on. It adapts by robbing Peter to pay Paul. At first, you may not notice these small deficits, which come in the form of:

1. Stress

2. Malnutrition (American is the most overfed, under nourished population.)

3. Lack of mobility causing structural issues in the spine and muscular degeneration. Lack of mobility and perspiration can also lead to a lack of ability to detox on a daily basis, as sweating is widely known to be a way to detox the body.

4. Toxic environments including: lotions, soaps, and anything applied to the skin. (It absorbs approximately 60% of what you put on it and it is the largest organ.)

The body needs energy and nourishment to survive. Our diet has changed drastically in the past 100 years and these changes have not been in our or the future generations' favor. The way to reverse this is to learn to make food healthy again. By plugging into the past, it is my belief that we can restore our gut health and ultimately our entire health. For this very reason, we created *The Cultured Collective*, our online fermentation business which teaches you how to ferment foods to unlock their nutritional value. By learning to connect with and make our own food in specific ways, health is attainable once again. Why did our ancestors ferment? It was simply out of necessity and survival in order to preserve the food. Little did they know the digestive benefits and healing powers of this art.

So what happened to the human race and health? Basically, we got greedy and fast food and TV dinners became popular. Before we knew it, the food we were eating began to look less like real food and more like a McDonald's Big-Mac that can sit on a counter without mold for over two weeks. Our highly processed foods take a toll on our bodies and if continued long enough, can contribute to catastrophic damage. If you do not make the time right now in your life to consume real food, I promise there will a day in the future when disease is at your doorstep, and you will be forced to make health your main focus. By then, you will wish you had slowed down to learn about healing your gut and life.

I delve much deeper into physical health and healing for the gypsy bod in a separate book for those of you who would like to explore it more deeply. It will cover the inner thoughts and feelings that aren't typically vocalized, changing the way you look at food and health. It can also affect how you interact with others as well as provide you with all of the facts about food and nutrition that you will ever need to know. It provides an unbreakable foundation of health so you can jump into your own self-discoveries, free to explore and flourish within this empowering dimension of nourishment and energy.

My journey with food, nutrition, emotions, healing, anxiety, and depression is one that is far too typical these days. To sum up my entire decade long journey in one chapter is impossible, that is why I decided to write an entire book on the subject matter. Here I will explore the body, nutrition, movement and true health at a deeper level. I'm excited to share with you the many lessons that I learned through trial and error. It's a journey that takes a lot of compassion and a strong desire to learn, but I believe with awareness and knowledge, you can begin to take responsibility for your own health.

For some of you, this one chapter will be all you need to optimize your health. For others who tend to internalize a lot of emotion or simply love to learn about health, you will need more. If you want to get a baseline of my philosophy in a fun, short way, you can visit iTunes for our *Gypsy Bod Health Hacks*. This is a 30-day challenge on my Gypsy Fam podcast. There are free, short 15-minute episodes where Charles and I break down important fundamental truths about health.

The food you put in your mouth and the energy it was *prepared with* matters more than you know. Your body's ability to digest and absorb food is the way you feel energy.

Want more energy? Heal your gut and you will absorb more nutrients and have more energy, feel better, and stay healthy! Answer the questions below.

<u>Action Exercise:</u>

- What 3 foods can you cut out?
    1._____
    2._____
    3._____

- What 3 foods can you increase?
    1._____
    2._____
    3._____

- What foods are you consuming that are most likely causing an inflammatory response in your body?
    1._____
    2._____
    3._____

- Hop online to the Health Hacks guide found at www. GypsyFam.com/GypsyLivingTips.
    What 3 things have you learned?
    1._____
    2._____
    3._____

The body is meant to move.

1. What is your health goal?

    _____
    _____
    _____
    _____
    _____

2. If you wrote anything about "pounds" go back and redo it. Health is not about the pounds on the scale.
3. Work on loving yourself each morning just the way you are.
4. Find a workout you love. Keep searching until you find it. When it loses its luster, find a new one and keep active, always.
5. Be active 7 days a week. Move your body, walk, dance, skip, or jump. Do what you can do to move your body more and sit less.

6. Get your heart rate up, sweat. A good rule of thumb is to get your blood pumping and sweat 20 minutes a day.
7. Cross-train and change up your exercises for muscle confusion.
8. Play like a child. Scramble around if you can, get on the ground, and never stop doing the moves you like.
9. Do yoga. If you can breathe, you can do yoga.
10. Do more yoga. Rehabilitate your body, your mind, and your spirit.

These tips will keep your body young like your gypsy spirit. The energy created by bringing in both healing foods and daily movement into your life will serve you and those around you every day in each moment. And when life is at its worst, you will know where to turn and the steps to take to regain your health.

Action Exercise:

• What exercise do you like/love currently that you could do 5-7 days a week for at least 20 minutes?

_____

_____

_____

_____

_____

• What will change if you don't?

_____

_____

_____

_____

_____

- What will change if you do?

  _____

  _____

  _____

  _____

  _____

- How does movement enhance your life?

  _____

  _____

  _____

  _____

  _____

- How does sweating and working out make you feel?

  _____

  _____

  _____

  _____

  _____

- Can you take the 30-Day online Gypsy Bod Health Hack challenge? Why is this important for your health?

  _____

  _____

  _____

  _____

  _____

Back in the primal times, man moved in many different ways—climbing, running, and rolling. We no longer move this way, nor do we eat the way we are meant to. Imagine what can open up for your body, mind, and spirit if you began moving and eating how you were meant to.

For more tips and tricks in health and fitness, check out my online resources, go to www.gypsyfam.com/GypsyLivingTips.

THE MIND

Let's move onto the mind. The hardships of the mind may seem like the hardest prong of the trifecta to overcome. The mind's voices can play tricks on us, therefore, not surprisingly, many of us get caught in the trap of listening to everything the mind says or "thinks" it feels.

Simply put, we are not our minds nor our thoughts. In today's environment with an abundance of technological stimulation, our minds and thoughts rarely stop. This constant stimulation being streamed into our lives causes our brains to function differently than they used to. Frankly, we are dumber than we used to be because we do not have to use our brains to try to retain information as we used to. Because of this constant stimulation and lack of stillness, we crave double tapping and scrolling when it is not around. Many people have no idea what to do with themselves without technology.

I invite you to look at your mind from the seat of consciousness that we talked about in the *Reflections* chapter. Step outside of your body and mind, and disconnect from that part of you. Look at your mind from this new perspective. Take a seat in a nice comfy cushion right on top of your brain; we will call this the gypsy seat of consciousness. Look at your thoughts as they come and go, listen to the chatter that is going on, notice, realize, and become aware of all that goes on in that vast mind of yours.

Separating oneself enough to become open to experience the senses of the mind *is* the art of mindfulness and meditation. As my dear friend and mindfulness mentor, Julianna Raye, teaches thousands, once you can do that you can begin to label your experience. The reason I mentioned this in the *Reflections* chapter and again here is because it is imperative to learn to disconnect from your mind. This is how you free yourself.

Recently I had a conversation about technology and mindfulness with Julianna. It was a discussion on the brain and technology and how mindfulness can benefit us in this day and age. I loved what she said, so I have included it here.

"Teach people how to work with any experience, including feeling inundated by electronics by using the skills of mindfulness. Mindfulness helps people to down-regulate the amygdala, which is responsible for our fight-or-flight or freeze response. It also strengthens or thickens the pre-frontal cortex."

Why do we want to strengthen our pre-frontal cortex? Goodtherapy.org tells us that our brain develops from the back to the front, the front being the last to develop. The roles of our pre-frontal cortex include, but are not limited to, personality, complex decision-making, planning skills, focusing and organizing skills.

In a nut shell, we all want a strong, thick pre-frontal cortex. Having one assists us in making more thoughtful decisions and helps us focus better. Really it helps us in everything we do simply because we are able to process and internalize our world on a deeper more meaningful level.

A gypsy understands that in order to stay connected to the gypsy spirit it's essential to learn the art of disconnecting emotionally from the mind. The need to know, figure out, or control the outcome of your life leads to making decisions and acting on emotions that usually are not in line with our spirit. Ultimately, this creates a great amount of internal disaccord.

The art of "letting go" is a practice that the mind understands, and these words are often heard in the whisperings of the gypsy spirit. The mind, not the spirit, chooses to struggle. The mind, not the spirit, fights. The mind, not the spirit, many times leads your body and life into a place that you do not really want to be. The mind is full of logic, and while it has a place in your life and decision-making skills, following the brain's logic is the main culprit of your lack of fulfillment.

When you close your eyes and focus your attention on the back of the brain, you can see through your third eye in the center of your forehead. This is where your intuition is housed. The mind plays an integral part in your health. Previously, we talked about how you interpret your world through your endocrine system. One aspect of this "interpretation" is how our brain looks at life, experiences, successes, failures, stressors and such. In short, you have a choice to respond to life instead of reacting to it, and the way is through controlling your mind.

My friend Rachel recounts her experience with this practice. "I was reminded of a time when doing this shortly after falling ill. I was laying down doing a body scan meditation and I could feel my entire body vibrating under the skin. It was very disconcerting and a symptom of my poor health. After doing the scan, which took about 20 minutes, my body was completely silent and still. It was a very profound moment and testament to the power of meditation."

This practice is powerful, and so are you. For more tips hop on my website.

THE (GYPSY) SPIRIT

Your gypsy spirit is meant to lead with its heart wings. Your gypsy wonderment that makes you undeniably you, including your deepest and truest desires filled with light and love, are the essence of your gypsy spirit. Like the beat of the African drum, your spirit consistently (even when the beat may seem hidden or muted) beckons you to connect to your higher purpose.

The beat of your gypsy spirit is the beat that unites you and me to others across land and sea. As our beats join the rhythmic thump we unite as one, allowing each person to be unique in their own right. It is the deep understanding that we are all the same. When you look at me, I am merely a reflection of yourself and visa-versa. As we see ourselves unite and answer the beat of the rhythmic drumming, we see gypsy spirits that have been dormant for years, rise up. We see those who were once cold and distrusting begin to smile and sway with the beat. As the music of the drum brings us together, we see how each of us is interconnected in this web of life. Our actions rippling, for better or worse, through the divine matrix of the universe. Is it any wonder we gravitate towards our tribe?

Your gypsy spirit will lovingly and wisely govern and lead you if you let it. When you are in tune with her cries, hopes, dreams and fears, you are in tune with your deepest intuition. Your intuition will always steer you well, for as you learn to follow the spirit you will notice that you make decisions from your own wisdom instead of others. As you begin to embrace your own unique beauty, you will become comfortable with saying "no" to that which does not serve you. The more your life becomes aligned with your greatest desires, passions, and purpose you will experience more happiness and fulfillment than you have ever before.

If you simply allow your life to be led by your gypsy spirit—doing more of what you love and leading with your heart—you will become the person you are meant to be. As the body begins to reflect your inner peace from the mind and spirit, people will begin to see your value and your worth, just as you do now (or soon will).

Health is the ultimate trifecta of the body, mind, and spirit combined into one great transmission of energy, which flows from one into another, and then from you into the world. When all are in proper order—the spirit leading the mind and the mind leading the body—disease and internal disaccord cannot exist. As you live your life in strict adherence to your internal North Star, which is your consciousness and heart awareness, your health will transform. The place from which you make your decisions will be honest and pure and you will be able to feel the peace that resides within you as you align with the rhythmic beat of your tribe.

Your life will begin to manifest all that you desire and your health will become the source of your greatest strength, simply because you are choosing to follow your inner voice and keep the trifecta of health in perfect alignment. Your body will begin to transform with needless weight melting off as you adhere to the *Gypsy Bod* guidelines. Weight loss is not a goal in itself, but a byproduct of living your life this way. The weight is not the problem, nor has it ever been, it is merely a symptom of the problem. This problem is solved through education, awareness, and empowerment. When you focus on the principles in this chapter, you focus on the roots of your health.

By taking this approach, you will see the trifecta of the body, mind, and spirit as the governing head. Looking at your own health, through this lens, can you see some areas you can improve upon? Go ahead and write 3 of them down.

_____

_____
_____
_____
_____

Your health is the key to your life. If there is one area to concentrate on, it is your own vitality and then, those you love. It is easy to let this aspect of our lives go and concentrate on other areas, which seem more fun and rewarding. You have the choice each day to live the life you want. Others have died so that you may have this beautiful life with all the freedoms you enjoy. What kind of life will you commit to living?

_____

_____

_____
_____
_____

How will you feed and nourish this beautiful physical representation of your life?

_____
_____
_____
_____
_____

How will you connect to the energies of the Universe and move your muscles, tendons, bones, and cells?

_____
_____
_____
_____
_____

What will you do today with your body that millions of others cannot? Be free.

_____
_____
_____
_____
_____

We scratched the surface of health in this chapter. For those of you who are ready to invest in your health and want the information now go to my website and click on my guide program. In this series of 6 week courses, The Body, The Mind, The Spirit are the foundation of my guide program. In order to work with me these courses must be completed as they set the foundation from which all flourishing and unleashing naturally evolve. I encourage you to follow your gypsy spirit to know the next best step for you.

DOODLE PAGE

XIV

"Y" is for your true value

"Owning our story can be hard but not nearly as difficult as spending our lives running from it. Embracing our vulnerabilities is risky but not nearly as dangerous as giving up on love and belonging and joy—the experiences that make us the most vulnerable. Only when we are brave enough to explore the darkness will we discover the infinite power of our light."

—BRENÉ BROWN

Your true value. What is your true value? Think about your life and what it would be like without you in it. What would change for those still living? Who would laugh more or less? Who do you see grieving for you and why? Most likely, the image of your life, without you in it, brings a tear to your eye. It does for me. I think of my husband who is my world. My kids who make up the bulk of my day and schedule. I think of their little faces as I kiss them goodnight. I think of my family and friends, and the thousands of people I have worked out with personally and through conferences and classes.

The value we give to others many times is the way we interpret our own worthiness and even, our true value. While I agree with adding value to others' lives, it is far different than the simple concept of understanding your true value. You are valuable, just because you are. Even with no rhyme or reason, you are a human, on earth, with value. You have value to offer and share with other humans and your experiences are important. The path you have traveled may have some dark spaces, we all have those. Yes, some of you more than others. For those of you who have darker spaces than most, have compassion on your journey and know that it has been for a reason. Possibly some inner turmoil that you have not been ready to deal with or understand. Those experiences do not make you worth less than me or anyone else. It is in the willingness to explore the dark spaces, as Brown talks about above, which can help us find the source of our own light.

Why? How? How can going into the problems of your life help you uncover your true value? Because where there is light, there can be no darkness. Darkness is shame, guilt, and unworthiness. Lightness is love, belonging, and joy (our first chakra). Your infinite power of your light comes through your ability to be vulnerable. Vulnerability allows us to be hurt because we lead with our heart, with love, and love is something we all crave. Once burned by love and vulnerability, coldness and darkness creep in and it becomes easy to live like the woman in my first poem, who chose the love of a rich man over true love.

The best way I can explain this is when I dance on stage. I do not know why or how, but leading people on stage in dancing and fitness is something that comes naturally, as if I was born to do it. It is a euphoric feeling for me. Not because I am on stage under lights, but because it is a powerful position to lead, to evoke movement from others, and to create something magical together that is larger than the sum of its parts.

Recently at The Best Year Ever conference, I met a man named Lance Carter, a tri-athlete who has finished many full and half iron-mans. At the beginning of the conference, I got the crowd moving. We had fun—we danced, we moved, and we broke down the shell that many of us walk around with in our daily lives. For me, I was simply "doing my thing."

Afterwards during the break, Lance walked up to me and gave me a huge compliment. He agreed to do a testimonial on my video and when we were finished, he grabbed the microphone and told the entire conference that he could go home right now. He offered that seeing me dance and lead in that way was exactly what he had needed at the conference. He now understood what it was like to play full out, to show up, and to not hold back in life.

Lance saw my ability to be vulnerable and celebrated it. People could have laughed at me. They could have all sat down and not participated, but they didn't. Why? Because people never do that with me. When people are in front of me and there is music, we move! People follow my lead because I was born to lead and create that energy. Could it be this strong belief of mine? Absolutely. Which stems from my confidence and knowledge that I am a valuable key to conferences and movement. I move people physically so they can be moved emotionally.

Lance may have wondered who I was when I first started moving and shaking. Most likely, he himself felt funny shaking his hips and probably felt a little awkward at first. It didn't take long for him to get lost in the movement and forgot about his own insecurities. Isn't that wonderful that he allowed my gifts to be transmitted so we could make magic!

Movement, energy, and love transforms us into the creators we truly are. We breathe, let go of feeling less than we truly are, and from there we can build. From a place of love and vulnerability, we can explore the darkness and shed the light. And where there is light, there can be no darkness.

The old Lance would have never had the courage to come up to me, let alone be on a video and speak in front of hundreds of people, but the new Lance did. My gypsy spirit awakened his gypsy spirit and his value came alive that day. He left that conference, and put this whole story into a book called, *Live Big*. All from being vulnerable and taking many big risks, that paid off. Light radiates from your gypsy spirit when you embrace your true value and allow it to lead.

Your true value is exponential and your worth magnificent. Although you are not above any other soul on Earth, nor are you below. Your true value has nothing to do with the numbers in your bank account or the home you live in. It is not based on your family dynamic or the place you were born. Your true value now (and has always been) something inherent inside of you.

Do you understand your true value?

Action Exercise:

- Do you feel valued? Why or why not?

  _____
  _____
  _____
  _____
  _____

- How do you feel valued?

  _____
  _____
  _____
  _____
  _____

- Who in your life values you?

  _____
  _____
  _____
  _____
  _____

- If you do not feel valued, it is because you must first value yourself. From where do you gain your value?

  _____
  _____
  _____
  _____
  _____

- Do others value you for your skills, looks, and exterior efforts?

  _____

_____

_____

_____

_____

- Do you in turn value others by what they "do" instead of who they "are?"

_____

_____

_____

_____

_____

- Name 3 people who value you just for being you.

_____

_____

_____

_____

_____

By divine right (or simply being born), your true value is infinite and the key to creating your future. By embracing how unique you are, you begin to see your worth more clearly. You already have gifts that make you unlike any other. When you honor your worthiness and what you want in life, you naturally open up to your strengths and talents.

Action Exercise:

- Name 3 talents or gifts you have. I know you have them, do you?
  1. _____
  2. _____
  3. _____

- What could you do with your talents?

  _____

  _____

  _____

  _____

  _____

- What could you do with your life that would allow you to fully embrace your talents?

  _____

  _____

  _____

  _____

  _____

When you learn to cultivate these gifts we call "talents," you will naturally excel. Your efforts may not feel like effort, and your actions may seem second nature to you. You may even think, "This is too easy!" By combining your true value with your talents and all we have been harnessing, you will have found your gypsy spirit key. This key unlocks the abundance that life has in store for you.

What is the key made of? You, your true value, and your awareness of it, which begins to shine through you in every act, word, and deed that you do. Your true value is more than sheer confidence, and it runs deeper than humility. This unbreakable assurance is inextricably rooted in the ways of the gypsy spirits that connect us as a whole. This beautiful way of living consciously aligns you with your dreams and your corresponding actions.

Your gypsy spirit is close to becoming unleashed. Can you feel it? With this final aspect of awareness of your true value, you will understand just how WORTHY you really are.

There is no denying that you have a gypsy spirit inside of you, and you can no longer deny that your true worth is magnificent. How is it that some crawl out of depression, and others do not? Simple, it is like my friend Tuan Ngueyn (C0-creator of *Let's Hug it Out*) mentioned on my podcast, it comes down to accountability and inspiration. We need to continually hold ourselves accountable for our dreams by continually remaining inspired. When we have someone or something to answer to, we rise up. When we are around people who lift and inspire us, we cannot help but think bigger and more brightly.

Your true value is more than you realize. *You* are bigger and brighter than you realize and hopefully, you now understand the influence that others have on you. On the flip side, if you are in an environment that does not support your dreams and goals, it is time to take a hard look at making some decisions to honor your true value. When you understand how valuable you are, you will not settle. When you "get" how awesome you are, you understand how much goodness there is in store for you! When you have to answer to an accountability partner or Gypsy Guide, you are many times more likely to show up. Why? Because it is in our nature to show up for others more than for ourselves. (Although, I hope you have been practicing and become a pro at putting your wants and needs first lately.)

Recognize that it takes daily practice for this beautiful message to become second nature. Eventually, it will be a part of you and you will never again think anything other than YOU ARE W.O.R.T.H.Y! You are unique, special and imperfectly you. You are wise, and able to focus on your one thing, reflect on your life, trust life, and understand your true value. In short, while the world is up to stuff, you will be up to something bigger!

It is time to show up in a bigger way for yourself. It is time for you to claim what you want and let go of debilitating beliefs about what is and is not possible for you. Breathe, relax, and let it all go. Choose to create in the future instead of letting fear control you because of the past. Choose you. Choose life and happiness. Choose to let go of what you cannot change so you can evolve and grow.

My intention is for you to be able to fully understand the worth of your gypsy spirit, and the necessary tools to practice to unleash that spirit to live an extraordinary and adventurous life! From this day forward, you are reminded of what it means to be a G-Y-P-S-Y who is filled with gratitude, is a yes for herself, is about positive purpose, loves herself, and is young at heart.

We are ready to move onto the next segment of the book. In this next section, we will dive into your roles and mission in life. We still have a part of your journey to travel and this next phase may test you. It is necessary to look inside and see what you are made of. Luckily, we already know all the good stuff that you have inside. Keep in mind that you currently have a life you've previously unconsciously created and quite possibly along with it, a few challenges that you must move through in order to live your adventure.

What has opened up for you in this chapter? What feelings are stirring inside of you? Write about your light and where it has been hiding.

DOODLE PAGE

PART 3

XV

gypsy roles

"The roles we play in each other's lives are only as powerful as the trust and connection between us--the protection, safety, and caring we are willing to share."

—OPRAH WINFREY

Now that you have a clearer view of your true value, I believe you will be able to look at the roles you play in your life with an unclouded lens. You also understand the foundational characteristics of a gypsy, and the daily rituals that you must align with in order to create the gypsy you want to become. You can become anyone you choose. You can create any life you can imagine. Although you have all of the information, you must be fully willing to implement it so you can change your behaviors and thus, change your life. By doing so, relationships and the roles that we have played in others' lives will be either reinvented, strengthened, or completely diminished.

What roles do you play in your own and in others' lives? Look at the life you have chosen—your family, friends, religious beliefs, communities, volunteer work, careers, and so forth. You have made choices, and those choices brought you to this place, at this moment. From this day forward, you know the importance of intentionally creating your life. To do so, you need to take a closer look at the "roles" that you play.

Action Exercise:

Make a list of 5-15 activities and the roles you play in them:

Mine looks like this:

- Wife
- Mother of 3 beautiful humans
- Gypsy Spirit
- Author
- Adventure, Explorer, Wanderluster
- Yoga lover, Baptiste Yoga Community
- Fitness and Nutrition Explorer, Instructor, Coach/ Guide, CPT
- Beach extraordinaire
- Friend
- Speaker
- The Cultured Collective, co-creator
- Ava Maria Lambs, co-creator
- Conference Speaker & Presenter (For example: the Best Year Ever Blueprint and Mommies Hiring Mommies)

You get the picture. You can also add volunteer opportunities, running, coffee lover, or tennis. List it all!

ACTION EXERCISE:

_____
_____
_____
_____
_____
_____
_____
_____
_____
_____

Then:

1. Go to the above list and mark 1-10 in order of importance with 1 being the most important.
2. Then go through and cross of anything that you do *not* love and are still a part of. (Keep the husband and kids, and those good to you!)

Note:

There may be aspects of identifying your most important roles that provide you with the opportunity to question what you are a part of and where you are going. The roles you play and the endeavors you align with change over the years as your life changes and your family dynamic shifts. Have you changed with it? Are you present in your life? You too have the ability to shift. Change and update your roles to ensure that you are committed to what is most important to you currently.

When making choices for your life ask yourself: Does this make sense? Does this choice feel good? If one role takes away from the higher priority roles, the answer becomes an automatic "no." By saying "no" to what you would normally say "yes" to, you will stay closer aligned to the life you desire. By doing less, you can absolutely accomplish more *and* you will maintain focus on what is truly important to you. This is how you live consciously and intentionally.

A note of caution, watch out for the word "busy." Busy is an under-descriptive, overused term for "I am doing a bunch of shit that I really don't want to be doing, but I do it anyway. I am worn out, tired, stressed, and need someone to acknowledge all that I do." You might as well say, "Thank you very much, I am totally and utterly unfulfilled." When I hear the word busy, that's what pops into my mind. Whose fault is it? Where can the finger be pointed? Only one person can take responsibility for your life, and that person is you. Do it. Own your life. Take responsibility and live in your power in the light, instead of in the shadows.

In order to unleash your gypsy spirit and live your most daring adventure, I want you to think about what you really want to create in your life.

Action Exercise:

Put your roles aside (I.E. - wife and mother).

Write down your "one thing." The one thing that you want to do above anything else, for you and only you.

Is it learning gymnastics? Is it your career or starting your own line of clothing? Is it planning your next adventure or financial freedom? What is it for you? What is it that haunts your happiness? What is the one thing that if you could, you would concentrate all your energy on?

Choose just one.

My "one thing" is:

_____

_____

_____

_____

_____

Too many roles allow you to get distracted easily. Do you tend to lose focus? That is the norm in today's high-tech driven world. Keep in mind social media is communication, not connection. The mind likes to be free and enjoys distractions so it is more difficult to focus rather than allow your mind to wander into other realms and activities. When the mind wanders, so does your life. Wandering through life is much different from a gypsy who wanderlusts. Be sure to choose carefully which hats you wear and what you focus on.

If this seems hard, just start with small tasks like working out. Plan it, and then do it. The more you plan and follow through, the easier staying focused will get. Workout your "get it done" muscle and pretty soon, you will be living intentionally and your life will begin to transform.

Right now, choose your highest priority and live in alignment with that priority. It is okay to put other goals on the back burner while you achieve your "one thing." So do it, write it down, post it where you can see it, and get it done. Afterwards, go to the next thing. Soon, you will surprise yourself with the realization that the fewer roles you have, the easier it is to focus and the more you will accomplish. The more you accomplish in the area you desire, the closer you will get to your goal. Before you know it, you will hit the mark and achieve your most important priority! Suddenly dreams become a reality, your fire will begin to burn, and no one will be able to stop you, all because you have less roles, less hats to wear, and less people to please. Remember, do less and accomplish more.

Believe me, I get it. I know how it is to be a wife and a mother, feeling overwhelmed by the myriad of tasks that being a mother brings with it. The endless dirty socks on the floor and dishes in the sink. The parenting and the loving, and don't forget the husband. I speak from experience. I sometimes feel stretched so thin, because I tend to be a "yes" for everything and everyone. It can be difficult to find the boundaries of our roles, especially when they bleed into one another.

Here is an example that may help you. I wrote this book you are reading or listening to right now while living in Puerto Rico. As you can image, writing a book is not a one-time thing. It is like an art project, which requires layer after layer of attention. Once Charles and I had gotten this art project to a place that we felt good about, I found an amazing editor. After it was edited, I thought we were done. Nope. I knew I needed to go back through yet again and add some finishing touches to ensure my golden messages were being delivered exactly the way I wanted.

Then life happened. I dislocated my ankle, the washer and dryer broke, the toilet overflowed, and to top it off someone came into our condo at night (while we all slept) and stole

Charles' wallet and both of our laptops. A week later, some of my besties came to visit and before we knew it, we were back in Southern Utah getting our kids intentionally into school, dance, and reconnecting with friends and family. Not to mention that we were building a new home and a permaculture garden. I understand. Life. Roles. Sometimes the "one thing" we have chosen, (like writing this book) takes a back seat for a time. This will happen because we are constantly playing Tetris with our "one thing" and our chosen top priorities.

It is for this reason that you must take responsibility for remaining dedicated to accomplishing your priorities and *your* "one thing." If you need a quiet space to work like I do, get an office. If you want to be an artist, create a space that is conducive to doing that one thing. Remember, you are not alone. Your dreams are not too big; you simply need to create the space so you can accomplish them. When I say "them," I really mean "one." Do one thing at a time and then move onto the next thing. If you are like me, you want to do a lot in a little bit of time and generally bite off more than you can chew. I have learned to slow down and be a little more realistic with what I can accomplish with my time. For instance, I wanted to re-edit my book in one week, but it took a month. I have learned that my initial estimated time frames are about a quarter of the time it will actually take me. The lesson is that I can now better gauge my time and completion of projects by knowing myself a bit better. This allows me to do less and accomplish more, which leaves me feeling fulfilled.

When you align your body, mind, and spirit with only one thing, you will be living from your power—your greatest intention. That is why fulfillment for me is different than it is for you. My heart wants what it wants, and yours wants what it wants. Embrace this, your gypsy spirit is meant to be unleashed! Different situations, careers, circumstances, and events have a different internal meaning for you than anyone else. Recognize *your* needs and embrace your uniqueness.

You can now make decisions more easily because of the above information. If you are stumped—keep going, keep reading, and even re-read this book if you need to. That is exactly what I do. I read sections of books, even whole books, over and over again. It is like striking gold repeatedly. You may not be ready to accept a transfer of knowledge or wisdom today, but you may be tomorrow or next month. When you read it, feel it. Breathe it in and allow the knowledge to seep into the very fibers of your body. By doing so, you will feed your gypsy spirit and begin to uncover your life's mission.

What have you uncovered about your roles and what you truly want to be doing with your life?

_____

_____

_____

_____

_____

_____

_____

_____

_____

_____

_____

_____

_____

DOODLE PAGE

XVI

mission

*"To realize one's destiny is a
person's only obligation."*

—PAULO COELHO,
The Alchemist

Did you know it is your obligation to find, discover, uncover, and live in tune with the beautiful symphony of your life's mission? This is my desire for you, and I am committed to assisting you in this sacred discovery. Keep in mind this is *not* your job or career, but what you *are* at your very core. This is about living each day with purpose.

Your purpose is held within your gypsy spirit and once unleashed, you shall be one step closer to realizing what *it* is. Imagine those little golden nuggets of truth and light waiting within, longing to be discovered. The time has come for you to uncover them. Not through hard-nosed determination and skepticism, but through willingness, openness, love, and self-acceptance.

You have chosen the top priority for your life. Is that really the most important priority you want in your life? Be curious and stay open. You are a creator, and as such, you were meant to live in alignment with your gypsy spirit at all times, in all places, and in each moment of your life. The time has come to claim your life mission.

What can you discover right here and right now about yourself that you will never find out there in the world? You can only appreciate adventure and discovery when you have first uncovered your inner truths about your desires, hopes, fears and what truly makes you unique.

The internal explorations of the gypsy spirit can be just as exciting as the outdoor explorations. From my experience, the internal adventure can be even more exhilarating than jumping from an airplane or running naked on the beach (both of which I have done more than once). When you realize your inherent goodness and worth, it will leave you with a peace that can only be found within you. Think of it like the sunrise of manifestation of all you are and can create. A true gypsy realizes that the greatest adventure ever taken is the one within.

I am going to make a few assumptions about you. I know you are a good person and assume you have vision and an adventurous spirit. Now it's time for you to answer the question, what are you all about? What do you need to realize and uncover? What is your destiny?

_____

_____

_____

_____

_____

_____

_____

_____

_____

_____

After all, the only obligation in your life is to find your destiny, as Paulo Coelho tells us. So what is your destiny? What can you be more open with yourself about? Why were you put here on Earth right at this moment? Do you know?

_____

_____

_____

_____

_____

_____

_____

_____

_____

No one else can figure this out for you, only you can. It is up to you, and I *am* here to assist you on this journey should you need my help. I want to help you design your dreams and uncover the disempowering beliefs that are making them difficult for you to see. What I've discovered is that my destiny is to help you align you with yours. You now know how to do it, so go ahead and do it! Own it and let this be the last time you waiver. Be honest with yourself and go after your destiny. Start today, this second, and don't waste another minute!

To discover your life's mission do what you love. Then, do more of what you love. Find ways to do even more of what you love. Keep searching for things you love about life. Stop trying to make everything happen or figure it all out, and simply let more of what you love find you. Whenever I hear myself or others say the words "I need to figure it out," I call attention to it.

I pause and I tell them (or myself) "actually, no, you do not need to figure anything out. All you really need to do is allow. Breathe, let go, let the mind relax, and turn your attention inward to your intuition—your gypsy spirit." Most likely, you already know what to do, where to go, or what to say "no" to. The head likes to confuse us. It is the ultimate simulator and is there for a reason, but surely not to lead. We have all done that and we know that following the head does not lead to fulfillment.

The heart is what leads us into the flow of our life. Find your flow. If you feel like you have been searching and you're worn out, then your spirit is tired and you need to restore. This happened to me in 2013. I was already at my limit and we had just moved back to Southern Utah from Arlington, Virginia to restore a trampoline business *and* begin another fitness business, as mentioned previously. After six months, I reached an all-time burn out and closed the business. For a few years, I concentrated on my family and me. By stopping and pulling back from my outward dreams, my introspective journey began, which clearly connected me to my life and eventually my purpose. In short, I let go of what I thought I had to do in order to become a "success" and in the process, truly came into my own. The journey to becoming me was one of the most pinnacle experiences of my life. It taught me what unleashing my own gypsy spirit was all about, and the struggle that we sometimes go through in order to unleash it.

Never underestimate your gypsy spirit. It will drive *and* govern you, and if you're true to it, it will never lead you astray. Believe in yourself, in your intuition, and allow this confidence to lead you to your mission. Your mission in life can take time, so be patient. One of the best pieces of advice that I can give you is an example from my own life. I have always lived with an open heart which made me work extra hard on learning to create boundaries in my life.

It is difficult for me to describe, but the best way I can say it is, "I've always felt there is something big for me to do." Money is not what drives me, although I will be the first to tell you that if your idea or mission is not profitable, it will never be sustainable. The next key point comes from a man who continues to amaze me, Jeff Hoffman, co-creator of Priceline.com. He said, "Never feel bad about making money. The lives you can and will bless with that money are far more than you can do without."

Many people have money issues. I find it usually stems from the way they were brought up. If this is your experience, you can massively benefit from *Secrets of the Millionaire Mind,* by T. Harv Eker. Do not let money be the thing that keeps you away from your life mission. Money is never the reason, nor should it be your excuse for living small. You are capable and you are worthy of all you want to create. So get going.

I want to take a moment to thank you for being a part of my life's mission. I am so grateful for your willingness to become introspective and for allowing me to guide you through unleashing your gypsy spirit so that you, and possibly your family, can live a more fulfilling and adventurous life. I cherish this role and want you to know how much I love this relationship with you.

Some of the information I am sharing with you may seem contradictory, as some of my words beckon you to go and do, while others may say to stop and breathe. Unleashing your gypsy spirit is a dance. At times, the dancing is slow and other times fast. Sometimes you fall down, and other times you are twirling in the air. Don't resist the dance, flow with the dance, life, and your intuition. Once you have unleashed your gypsy spirit, there is no need to worry because you will be in tune with you, and that is all you need.

What is opening up for you about your life's mission?

_____

_____

_____

_____

_____

_____

_____

_____

_____

_____

_____

_____

_____

_____

_____

_____

_____

_____

_____

The following will assist you in creating your life mission statement. Fill in the blanks...

The Gypsy Life Mission Outline:

My name is _____.
I am committed to living a life full of _____.
My Gypsy Spirit is a creator of _____ and I
will _____ all things that are _____,
_____ and _____to that end. I will concentrate
on _____ and align myself only to those gypsies who
_____, _____ and _____ me to be
_____. I will create _____
for my life and am committed to _____ by
_____ date.

An example:

Note that I could have published *Gypsy Living* by my goal date. I chose to make what I produce exceptional so this took me longer than expected. Dates are great but some goals will take longer to accomplish. The point is to not always hit the date, but to continually move forward achieving our dreams.

This will help you get started. Scan and print it, fill it in, and hang it up where you will see it at least three times a day. When you read it, really feel it, visualize it, and see your gypsy spirit gain assurance, confidence, and momentum. Think about this as you wake up and as you retire every day. The power held within you is so much more influential than you realize.

Your destiny is waiting for you. You can take your entire life to get there (if you want) and you will if you don't get started! It is time to begin and enjoy the ride knowing that you are headed to an intentional destination of your choosing. Remember, let go of the need to control the outcome of that destiny by setting your goals and priorities while staying flexible. Your life mission is not a science, it is an art and you have everything you need to begin your journey.

Are you ready? Is anything holding you back? This is a big step. If you are overwhelmed take your time and re-read or let this information settle inside of you for a while. Write about your feelings.

_____

_____

_____

_____

_____

_____

_____

_____

_____

_____

_____

_____

_____

_____

_____

_____

_____

_____

DOODLE PAGE

XVII

unleash your gypsy spirit

"She was born to be free, let her run wild in her own way and you will never lose her."

—NIKKI ROWE

BORN TO BE FREE

You *are* free, especially now that you've embraced your wild and adventurous gypsy spirit. From the understanding you've gained from the previous chapters, you know there is a paradigm shift that is taking place. Are you able to see more clearly where the beliefs you were previously living by came from?

_____

_____

_____

_____

_____

_____

_____

_____

The journey I have taken you on thus far has led you to a crossroads, and it is now your choice where you will go.

Have you chosen your journey with intention? In this moment, you are faced with the option of unleashing your gypsy spirit, or staying the same as you were before. Although, not fully, because you've already changed irreversibly as you read my words and felt the truths in you stir. Remember, I am asking you to move through a lot of phases, so if you are not ready, take a break and listen to the book again. Only you know when you are ready. There will be a day when you are ready to take a deep breath and take a leap of faith.

Although you were born free and have always been, you previously chose to tie yourself down. I hope through the work we've done, there is little left that makes you feel this way. If there is still something or someone that has you feeling tied down, be open and honest as you communicate your feelings with them. When you come from a place of love and compassion with that person, and if that relationship is worthy of you and you of them, healing and repairing damage can happen rapidly. Take the time to get back on track and heal with love.

Do you need to address something or someone here?

_____

_____

_____

_____

_____

_____

_____

Typically, we have resentments towards our parents for things that they *did* or did *not* do. It's important to bring awareness into this space and fully own it. Addressing these feelings can be difficult, I know.

Many of us deal with this undertaking somewhere between our mid-20's to our mid-40's because as we age, we gather wisdom that allows us to see what we couldn't in our younger years. Along with space comes clarity, therefore, we are more able to forgive, realizing that we are all just big kids doing our best. This helps us learn to respond instead of simply reacting within these relationships.

Most of my family and friends have "issues" with their parents. As children, many life choices were made for us, and that can be difficult for many of us. Let's revisit when you were a child to see how you felt.

<u>Action Exercise:</u>

- What did you most wish for as a kid?

  _____

  _____

  _____

  _____

  _____

- What did you hate or struggle with? You now have the power to forgive your parents and those who possibly wronged you. More importantly, you have the power to forgive yourself for allowing this darkness to continue to influence your life and your own choices. Nothing has power over you, nothing.

  _____

_____

_____

_____

_____

- What darkness have you allowed to have power over you?

_____

_____

_____

_____

_____

- Why?

_____

_____

_____

_____

- What aspect of living with that darkness is serving you?

_____

_____

_____

_____

- What are you gaining by living with this excuse?

_____

_____

_____

_____

- Can you forgive, let it go, and choose to move on?

  _____

  _____

  _____

  _____

  _____

- What actions will you take if you fall back into this old mental habit? (Pick a favorite song, splash water on your face, or something crazy that will get you out of the slump QUICKLY!)

  _____

  _____

  _____

  _____

  _____

If your career is tying you down and income is the main issue, then address it and make note of how you feel. This work can be a challenge! However, I have confidence in our relationship and I know that transformations can transpire through the connection that we have built. You have the ability to allow my words to transcend time and space and to heal your wounds and your life. I believe this because I believe in you and I know that your gypsy spirit is worthy of becoming unleashed. If you have failed, simply smile because life is always filled with second chances.

YOU ARE MEANT TO BE FREE. IT'S TIME TO UNLEASH!

From this day forward, vow to stop living a life of comfort. Stop lying to yourself. It is time to allow yourself to live from your heart and soul—your gypsy spirit. You are free from judgement, worry, malice and anything else that does not serve you. Unleashing cannot happen until you break free from the chains that you put in place.

Close your eyes and listen, or if you are reading, read the next paragraph and then pause to let these words gather in your heart so they can fully sink in.

My beloved, you are a gypsy. You are now free, and today marks your rebirth. Today you cut the cord that has allowed other people and "things" in your life to hold you down. Beginning today, you choose your freedom and the ties that have bound you are gone.

Open your eyes. Take a deep breath.

Why is this so important, right here, right now? What is the urgency? Your life, your happiness, and your fulfillment are waiting for you once you do. The time is now and it is time to imagine your way there.

While that little exercise was fun, you may not completely understand the weight of this moment in your life. Wake up! Imagine that you *must* unleash your gypsy spirit. There is no other option!

<u>Visualization Exercise:</u>

My intention with this heart-wrenching story is to help you realize how deeply you must desire these changes in your life. While the story may initially seem dark, so is the place where you store your hidden emotions and disempowering beliefs. It is only when we are able to shed light on these moments that we realize how light dispels all darkness, because where there is light, there can be no darkness.

Why Must You Unleash Your Gypsy Spirit?

Imagine you are on a cliff beside the sea. Just below is the daunting image of angry waves crashing on the rocky shore. Suddenly, you see your one-week-old baby chained to the rocks that will surely drag her to the bottom of the ocean. You want to save her, but as you move towards her you realize you are also in chains. It's torture because you are a mere two inches from being able to reach her.

The baby's death is imminent; can you free the chains that hold you down? Can you allow yourself the grace and compassion to let the past be the past and begin again? Can you face your deepest demons and allow your life to be fully lived right here and right now? Can you commit to living in the present with an open heart and a free spirit? Can you let go of remorse, regret, and resentment for yourself and others? As soon as you do, the chains that hold you and your baby to the rocks will disappear. *Now* can you? Would you be willing to lose yourself to find yourself?

While you are on this cliff, you don't know that this is how to save your baby so all that you think to do is scream. When you do, along with that vocal expression of self-doubt and victimization, the chains that will lead to your baby's death in the deep dark ocean, pull even tighter against the rough tides! The lack of understanding that you have about your power could cause the death of what you love most on this earth.

Will you become who you were meant to be? Are you willing to uncover the truth and look that baby in the eyes? Come out of hiding and release the façade that you have found comfort and solace in. The baby is fully in the arms of your captor and being prepared for heavens arms.

Look inside; feel the strength of the love and yearning you have to rescue this helpless baby. Of course, you want to. Every cell in your body, mind, and spirit are colliding into a burst of magnetic energy that make you feel as if you want to escape your body, escape these chains, and finally be free! With each inhale and exhale of your breath, your desire to be free so you can save your baby and yourself roots more deeply.

Look at your own feelings of frustration for not having the answers to your own life. Look at you! Look at the waves as they crash down mightily. Your baby will surely die as soon as one hits her. The anxiety, fear, and love makes you thrash at the chains and scream to the heavens and all the hells combined! As the wind beats upon your face and whips your hair back and forth, causing your skirts to fly up to the heavens, you know you must find a way! You think you may continue screaming out of rage, but you don't. Do you know that you do not have to think, analyze, or contemplate a rescue plan? The tumultuous emotions fill every cell of your body, pulsating passion through your veins. Then it happens. Time stands still. Suddenly everything stops.

You relax, slowly inhaling deeply, and then exhaling fully. As you narrow your gaze on your baby in one defining moment, you realize you will save her. You are the creator of your story and right now, you have the power to claim it! You realize this is all a simulation to allow you to go deeper into your present moment and to fully reclaim all of your gypsy spirit. Now you have tapped into your limitless confidence, connecting to the child inside that already lives through her gypsy spirit.

Suddenly, it hits you...you are the baby. This is you saving yourself, your legacy, and the best parts of you that are still inside and have yet to be discovered. You must find a reason for living for yourself—the sweet infant inside. You must know that you are worthy of the life you desire. As the light inside grows brighter, you don't quite understand it but you realize in this moment that you have created this scene, assigning a role to different parts of yourself. You may not have truly understood until you externally saw your own flesh and blood hanging in the balance, that all of the torment you felt were the cries of *your* tortured soul. It wanted to be free of the wind, the chains, and the captor that played leading roles in your life. Previously, you gave them power and meaning, but now the show is over.

In an instant, everyone and everything in this scene disappears. As the image of the cliffs fade away like a page from an ancient storybook, you look down and see your baby safely in your loving arms. You exhale as you realize you had the power all along. You always had the choice to claim your life, and by reclaiming it, everything in your world has changed.

Action Exercise:

You are powerful. You are a goddess of power and light. You are here for a reason with a purpose to fulfill. Allow that fact to encompass all of you. Take a deep breath and say it, yell it, scream it, or whatever you need to do. Go to the ocean cliff in your gypsy wear if you need and raise your hands to the heavens and yell, "I AM FREE! I CLAIM ALL THAT IS MINE AND MEANT FOR ME! I ACCEPT GREATNESS AND ABUNDANCE! THANK YOU!"

Yes, you are. Allow your tears to flow, and the freedom to seep into your soul. Take as long as you need and treasure this moment. You will always remember and cherish it as the day you chose to allow your gypsy spirit to be born again.

Welcome to your life my gypsy, my dear one; I have been waiting for you. You are now fully aligned with your gypsy spirit! With the unleashing of any physical, mental, and spiritual chains, you are now ready to live an adventurous and extraordinary life. I honor your journey and I'm smiling as I write these words, for you have so much life to live and share.

Action Exercise:

- Write continuously for 20 minutes about this experience. Don't worry about grammar or punctuation, just let it flow. Allow your feelings to come alive through this paper and ink. What are you unleashing? What are you letting go? What are you now able to create? Write it down.

ANDREA B. RIGGS

ANDREA B. RIGGS

DOODLE PAGE

XVIII

[ad-ven-ture]

"Security is mostly a superstition. It does not exist in nature, nor do the children of men as a whole experience it. Avoiding danger is no safer in the long run than outright exposure. Life is either a daring adventure or nothing."

—HELEN KELLER

ADVENTURE IS A GYPSY'S MIDDLE NAME.

Your gypsy spirit is now unleashed, or at the very least you are well on your way! This journey is a beautiful one filled with up's and down's. The most important aspect is to realize that either you *are* living your most daring adventure each and every day, or you *are not*. I believe you now have this awareness and I'm confident you are going to choose to live this way from here forward!

I want you to think of the word "adventure" as your new middle name because it will always remind you to turn a dark day into the best day of your life. By using this word, you will begin to see life as Helen Keller did—a daring adventure. Which is quite ironic, is it not? She was blind *and* deaf, which is probably why she "saw" every day as a daring adventure. In a way, she had no other choice. What if you had no other choice? What an epic journey her life turned out to be, displaying such strength and courage to so many of us, as told in books, school plays, and movies.

What if your world was dark, you couldn't hear, and people were grabbing you to try to communicate in completely different ways. Can you even imagine the struggle this poor child faced after she contracted a disease at nineteen months old, leaving her blind and deaf?

Each day when you want to complain, think about Helen Keller. Think about my friend Dan, who had his legs amputated after sustaining tragic wounds from war, yet he continues to inspire others through Baptiste Yoga. Think of the children all over the world who suffer abuses of every kind. Think of those that have it a 1,000 times worse than you do. Do we really have all that much to complain about?

Would we really trade in our "hardships" for another's? I heard my friend Jon Vroman, author of *The Front Row Factor,* say "if we were all sitting around and throwing our problems onto the table like dice, we would be quick to grab our own dice back." Adventure *is* born out of gratitude.

What does adventure mean to you?

_____

_____

_____

_____

_____

_____

How does the world define it? Merriam-webster Merriam-webster dictionary tells us:

1: an undertaking usually involving danger and unknown risks *a book recounting his many bold adventures*
   b: the encountering of risks *the spirit of adventure*
2: an exciting or remarkable experience
3: an enterprise involving financial risk

To me, adventure encompasses living your most daring adventure each and every day, for the rest of your life. Adventure is the deep-rooted hunger of your soul to seek, discover, and explore both your inner and outer worlds. It is the unquenchable curiosity to dig deeper into life's most exhilarating truths in the great jungles of Africa or even in your own kitchen as you make dinner. Adventure is having 100% faith in knowing the next event coming into your life is going to fill it with energy, connection, and wonderment.

Choosing adventure is an attitude.

So are you up for an exciting or unusual experience in which YOU will be the active participant, welcoming a BOLD and possibly somewhat risky outcome? Are you ready to live the spirit of adventure? Are you ready for a paradigm shift?

Welcome to this thing called "life" where nothing is set in stone and everything is up for grabs! As you seek new opportunities and adventures whispered to you by your gypsy spirit, you will begin to believe in yourself more and more. The more you embark on new adventures; you will see that trying is what life is all about. Sometimes those "tries" work out, and sometimes they do not. It is all for the good of the soul, to shape our gypsy spirit into those beautiful characteristics we have learned about.

As you learn to be led by your gypsy spirit, you will begin to live each day full of wonder, naturally ushering in more and more abundance. Resolve now to make the commitment.

Are you committed to a daily practice of honoring your gypsy spirit?

_____

How much time will you commit?

_____
_____
_____
_____

Where can you carve out this time? I.e. - getting up 20 minutes earlier or cutting out one TV show that you don't love.

_____
_____
_____
_____

Don't worry, you will slip up and some days will be better than others, so be driven with your intent and flexible in your approach. Remember, it is the culmination of your daily decisions that create your life. Commit to making each one great by doing it intentionally. "Going with the flow" does not mean floating aimlessly down the river. Gypsies do not float, but instead they seek adventure, using intent through a conscious heart and mind. They are led by spirit. They know that each gaze is a connection of spirit, and each internal intention set has universal organizing power that transcends from your heart into the cosmos.

You are ready! It is time to set an intention and choose adventure. It is okay to begin with little risks to see what it feels like to fall down and have a "failure." Before you know it, you will begin to call everything you want to do in life an adventure and you will be doing it every day, even if it is in a small way. This will teach you to laugh gently, yet easily, at yourself when you trip or fall. In fact, this will become a fun part of your adventure and some of the greatest lessons in your life.

Hint: A gypsy always chooses adventure. Allow the word *adventure* to glitter through your existence all day from morning until night. Incorporate this when teaching your children. Instead of getting it through video games, go outside more and be creative with seeking new experiences.

Action Exercise:

Here are a few tools to help you get started with seeking out adventure in the world:

1. Begin by going outdoors for 20 minutes a day without any distractions or electronics.
    a. Examples: Go on a hike, swing in a hammock and watch the clouds, play at a park with your children, go paddle boarding, kiting or explore the state and national parks around you.
    What are 3 actionable ideas that feel good that you want to implement?

1._____
2._____
3._____

2. Commit to going on a weekly outdoor adventure. Begin with setting aside one hour and work up from there.
   a. Examples: Go on a longer hike and pack a lunch. Hit the beach! Ask local friends some of their favorite places to explore near you. Invite a family on a 1-3 hour outing and loose the electronics. (My kids know that when we "adventure" that means no electronics. Car rides have evoked such meaningful conversations between our kids and us.)

   What are 3 actionable ideas that feel good that you want to implement?
   1._____
   2._____
   3._____

3. Once this feels good and you are enjoying it, move to the next outdoor adventure that inspires you.
   a. Examples: Learn something new together such as rock climbing, snorkeling, or scuba diving. Jump off small cliffs (safety always first please). Plan a trip to Colorado or come see me at Zion National Park here in Southern Utah. Plan the trips you have always wanted to go on. Live the life you have always dreamed of.

What are 3 more actionable ideas that feel good that you want to implement?

1._____

2._____

3._____

These examples may seem simple, and they are but they can change the way you live your life. By reflecting and continually challenging yourself and your adventure limits, you will see massive changes in your life. I promise.

Learning to play and let the mind go is as important as work. By allowing yourself the freedom to explore and lose track of time, your entire spirit relaxes. You begin to smile more, worry less, and enjoy life.

While you are enjoying your gypsy life more than ever, I would like to give you a few ways to avoid pitfalls. Here they are:

1. Front of Mind

Read or listen to this **once a month** to refresh. We are human and many of us read something and immediately go to the next thing. Stop. Use this as it is meant to and learn it, integrate it, and repeat. Repeat. Repeat. Repeat.

2. Worthy

Do the daily W.O.R.T.H.Y. exercises in the previous section. Your success depends largely on your ability to improve your gypsy mind and soul on a daily basis. We focus and stay the course, but remember to be flexible on the journey realizing that your meditation and practices may look different from others.

3. Commit

When you are ready to go on an adventure COMMIT. **Commit** by putting money down on a car, hotel, flight, or experience. Going beyond setting a date is imperative to get you moving down the trail.

4. Research

Research and think for yourself. You don't have to use a travel company. Dig deeper, find the deals and local's only hikes, beaches, and sites. Don't be a tourist, be a gypsy, and take the path less traveled. Keep in mind, a gypsy is a gypsy, not a tourist. Don't get mixed up in the ideals of the all-inclusive resorts (although this may be a great way for many to begin). So if this is you, embrace it! Adventure is usually minimal in this type of environment. The typical excursion is what everyone does because it seems easiest. You can be a gypsy and not stay in hotels with Airbnb, VRBO.com, Homeaway.com, home exchange sites, couch surfing and more, the traveling options for you are limitless and more affordable. And don't forget camping!

5. Stay Positive

Trouble will come and you will fail along the way. Shrug it off, keep your chin up, and stay happy and focused on why you are living this way. At first, it may seem difficult, but in time, you will be dancing and singing through troubles, even circumstances that would throw most into an internal whirlwind of despair. You will thrive in all situations and adventure will always follow you.

6. Prepare

Prepare items needed to go on your trip like a passport. If you need new clothes, which is doubtful because gypsies have a talent for using what they have or purchasing items on the go. Some supplies are easy to find cheap, others such as a tent or coats will be worth the expense. If you need new minimalist shoes or supplies, order them a month in advance and ideally have them delivered two weeks prior so you are not stressing about them. I love Patagonia, Osprey, Athleta, Lulu Lemon, Dakine, Billabong, Xero shoes, Roxy and more. For a more complete list and ways in which I am making my purchases more thoughtful and sustainable (eco-friendly) check out www.gypsyfam.com/GypsyLivingTips.

7. Enjoy and Experience

Joy. Happy. Fulfilled. Breathe. Meditation. Flourish and flow. These are the words that you will embrace and bring into your body and mind as you prepare and go on your adventure. Adventure is about including all of the happy words and feelings you can think of. Feel them in every cell of your body, in each task, moment, preparation, and travel experience, along with every word you utter.

TIP:

While traveling abroad, gypsies will search out affordable food joints that are delicious and many times more relaxing, cultural, and fun, not to mention easier on your wallet. Step outside your comfort zone and make friends by getting to know the locals. This will give you a taste for the local community, in addition to getting to know them! Strike up conversations with people, even if you can't speak their language. Connection often times does not need to have the same language. While living in Puerto Rico and learning Spanish, there were many times I had to fumble through my beginning Española! We just smiled and laughed. Remember, we are humans and are meant to connect and make a positive impact on each other's lives. Don't limit yourself.

By following these simple guidelines, you will ensure commitment and success in your adventurous future.

Secrets to making adventures extraordinary:

1-Listen or read this until it sticks.
2-Practice daily WORTHY skills.
3-Commit by solidifying a date and making the investment.
4-Research.
5-Stay Positive.
6-Prepare.
7-Enjoy!

What has clicked for you in this last chapter? Do you feel like living an adventurous life is closer than you thought? What adventures are you excited about?

_____

_____

_____

_____

_____

_____

_____

DOODLE PAGE

XIX

and you're off!

"You're off to Great Places!
Today is your day!
Your mountain is waiting,
So...get on your way!"

—DR. SEUSS, *OH, THE PLACES YOU'LL GO!*

I bet you have been waiting for this—planning the actual physical adventure. Travelling is closer than you think. Wow, look at you my gypsy sister, ready to explore! The caravans are waiting, your crazy gypsy hair tied up in curls and ribbons, your necklaces are jingling with excitement, and your bare feet are ready to absorb the fantastic earth energy. Yes, you really are ready—body, mind, and spirit.

As you gain more experience with attracting goodness and abundance by living aligned with your gypsy spirit, you will begin to notice your life easily becoming better and better. You will also notice that your intent will become more straightforward. Along with these changes, it becomes second nature to say "no" to others and distractions because you have a clearer vision of where you are headed.

Your daily dedication to implementing and practicing your internal tools has prepared you to take the next step—a real life, physical adventure! Big adventures to the sea, to the woods, to the mountains, to the jungles, and places no woman has gone before! Your time is now and you need to begin exercising your gypsy spirit's muscles.

The wonderful thing is, if you are already taking part in these adventures, with the tools in this book and the awareness you now have, you will be able to experience deeper fulfilment, connection, and gratitude than ever before. There will always be more caves to explore, and oceans to dive in. There is no peak for adventure and exploration, just more to learn, discover, and treasure. Just as these adventures wait for you, so does your internal one.

Charles and I are both outdoor people. That is not to say we do not sit at computers, we do, but we've known since our courtship that we were both committed to living life outdoors as much as possible. Next, I'm going to share the rules that work for us.

Here are 5 of our unwritten (now written) rules:

#1. Love nature.

We love nature and we love earth energy. Both of us crave exploring in the desert, mountains, hills, valleys, canyons, beaches, rainforests, and peaks. Discovering—whether it is shells, bugs, arrowheads or whatever gems lay hidden—is better than Christmas morning to our family. This is the first "love" to acquire and it takes a diligent effort especially in today's world. It is possible, however, initially you will need to research and plan before taking action. Soon, it will become second nature and the necessary items needed for your adventures will become increasingly easier to remember, purchase, gather, take, and clean-up.

Nature naturally helps you get in touch with your soul and your spirit. Personally, I believe that if you do not love nature, it may stem from a lack of self-love that is amplified when you are alone and surrounded by her beauty. We have talked about the importance of self-love previously and it will serve you well here.

The four elements—earth, wind, fire, and water—hold powerful healing energy that I believe are still the greatest healers of our time. This is undeniable when you walk through Southern Utah on the red sandstone, swim in the open ocean in Kauai, dance next to the bonfire in Puerto Rico, camp in Colorado, or simply let the wind hold you in her coattails. When you do, you will know peace that only comes from the awakening of spirit. This awareness aligns you with the magnificent power that is all around and within you.

Where are some places you've experienced this feeling in nature? When have you felt this energy?

_____

_____

_____

_____

_____

Where have you always wanted go and haven't?

_____

_____

_____

_____

_____

#2. Commit to feeding your soul like you feed your body.

When we lived in Washington D.C., Charles was usually unhappy. Really! My memories of him were bleak and it was for one simple reason, he felt trapped. You may be like him, or you may be more adaptable, like me. Either way, we must recognize that our soul wants what it wants and for many of us, it needs time and space in nature to unplug. Whether we love hiking, running, yoga, digging for gold, building a fort, or anything else, it doesn't matter as long as we have the freedom to create a way for our minds, bodies, and spirits to reset. Commit to feeding your soul like you feed your body by setting aside time for this. It should be one of your top priorities and always in the forefront of your mind.

Where does your gypsy spirit feel alive and free?

_____

_____

_____

_____

_____

How and where do you reset? How often do you give yourself this gift?

_____

_____

_____

_____

_____

#3. Teach your baby gypsies to love adventure.

Even if you don't have children of your own, you most likely, directly or indirectly, influence many mini-gypsies. I believe that women are mothers to many in a plethora of ways. If you are a woman, you "mother" simply because it is unavoidable as it is our nature to love and to nurture.

Why do our children swim in the open ocean, dive to the bottom of the sea, swing from vines, cliff jump, explore through jungles, hover over petroglyphs, climb trees, upcycle with boxes, cherish animals, and play for hours totally content in nature? Because they have always done it. As babies, our children ran barefoot on the red rocks of Southern Utah, eating dirt and staining their clothes. We let them play for hours in the water, and even let them put their bare feet in the freezing snow in the winter. We let them experience life.

Teach and allow your babies to explore and love nature. Teach them to love what you love because if you don't, one day you will wonder why you are so different from your children. The answer will be simple—you didn't model for them how to love what you love. Make the time and expend the necessary energy to create the connections that no amount of money can buy. Don't worry, embracing adventure transcends age so you can always establish this any time, however, it is much easier to do when they are young. Adventuring together helps establish a connection of unconditional love with your children, reinforcing that they can always come to you, no matter what.

In what ways are you teaching those mini-gypsies in your life to sink their teeth into adventure?

_____

_____

_____

_____

_____

In what ways are you hindering adventure with your little ones? In what ways can you overcome these challenges?

_____

_____

_____

_____

_____

In what ways have you already laid a great foundation for your family to begin to practice on a more conscious level?

_____

_____

_____

_____

_____

#4. Create time and space. It's never too late.

You always have time. Time to learn. Time to love. Time to explore. Time to be curious. Time to experience. Time to cry. Time to fail. Time to adventure. Time to live.

In Baptiste yoga, we teach our students to:

1. Be a Yes.
2. Give up what you must.
3. Come from a place of "you are ready now."

You can use these reminders:

1. Say "yes" to adventure now.
2. Give up all of the hang-up's that mentally tell you that you can't.
3. Come from a "you are ready right here, right now," place no matter what your perceived physical, mental, financial, or spiritual limitations may be.

Are you ready to begin living the life you want, right now? How can you integrate these mantras into your life easily?

_____

_____

_____

_____

_____

#5. Community

Who we rub shoulders with matters. Have you heard the statement that we are the compilation of the five people we spend the most time with?

Who are those five people in your life?
1. _____
2. _____
3. _____
4. _____
5. _____

Do you want to be like these 5 people? Why or why not?

_____

_____

_____

_____

_____

What can you do to ensure the 5 people you spend the most time with are the ones you really desire to be like? (Examples: Hire a guide, accountability partner, or join a community that uplifts and inspires you.)

_____

_____

_____

_____

_____

By now you know I am a part of many wonderful communities. Closest to my heart are those which I started such as The Cultured Collective and Gypsy Living.

How can *you* better show up for people?

_____

_____

_____

_____

_____

By aligning ourselves with others who embrace similar values, we recognize that we are not alone on our journey. We begin to accept help where we need it, and offer a hand to those we can serve. If you are in need of surrounding yourself with new people that are committed to living a life of adventure, the Gypsy Living Community can align you with people who can help lift you up, hold you accountable, and offer guidance.

This is so important that I am going to repeat it again... adventure begins with *your* attitude towards life. Begin changing it so you can start living the life of your dreams! Now that you are familiar with your 5 tools, you are ready to make your very own first ADVENTURE PLAN! How can you implement adventure? Simply begin with a plan.

As you strengthen your adventure muscles you will begin to get more and more daring. You will see your outings grow longer and trips that you normally would not have planned are now planned!

MY NEXT BIG ADVENTURE PRE-TRIP DETAILS

My next adventure is going to be epic!

Top 3 choices:
1. _____
2. _____
3. _____

I really want to go to one of these 3 places next because:
1. _____
2. _____
3. _____

Who will be coming with me?

_____

_____

_____

_____

_____

What will I do with kids, pets, and plants while I am gone?

_____

_____

_____

_____

_____

Do I need a house sitter? If so, who will this be?

_____

_____

_____

_____

_____

Will we drive or fly? What questions need to be addressed prior to departure? What items need to be purchased beforehand?

_____

_____

_____

_____

My tentative adventure date will be

_____.

*It is okay to put a tentative date here and pencil it in initially until you get travel arrangements, flights, car, and time-off dates solidified.

Research mode:

Research within one week. Reach out via text, calls, online, and Facebook with friends and family. What have you found out?

_____

_____

_____

_____

_____

Can you narrow it down to one destination? Where to sister?

_____

_____

_____

_____

_____

The date your research will be completed by _____.

Planned Budget Options:

1. Keeping it cheap, local, and fun.
2. Planning an out-of-state trip can cost from a few hundred to $1,000.
3. Going all out on flights & VRBO can cost anywhere from $1k-20k.

What is your budget for this adventure? _____

The most important aspect of this adventure for me is:

_____

_____

_____

_____

_____.

I am committed to making this trip the best ever by:

_____

_____

_____

_____

_____

Concerns I have?

_____

_____

_____

_____

_____

Research items?

_____

_____

_____

_____

_____

Hesitations?

_____

MY NEXT ADVENTURE

To help you plan your next adventure visit gypsyfam. com/GypsyLivingTips and click on *Adventure Ready* for a printable *My Next Adventure* Worksheet.

I know there are many of you who have not traveled much and may feel intimidated by the process as a whole. Currently, I am putting together my favorite gypsy travels, incorporating my favorite experiences, lessons, and how-to's.

DOODLE PAGE

XX

the extraordinary life of a gypsy

*"Do not ask your children to strive for extraordinary
lives. Such striving may seem admirable, but it is
the way of foolishness. Help them instead to find
the wonder and the marvel of an ordinary life.
Show them the joy of tasting tomatoes, apples and
pears. Show them how to cry when pets and people
die. Show them the infinite pleasure in the touch
of a hand. And make the ordinary come alive for
them. The extraordinary will take care of itself."*

—WILLIAM MARTIN

Most of us crave an extraordinary life—something better
than ordinary. Maybe for you, it is more happiness, money,
traveling, a bigger house, more kids, less kids, more fame,
more success, clothes, or more of this or that. You may not
even know what it means to live an extraordinary life; you
just know you don't have it.

As a young girl, I was lucky enough to travel quite a bit which helped awaken my gypsy spirit and her yearning to discover life's deeper meanings. I wanted an extraordinary life, however, I couldn't pin point exactly what "it" was that would make that a reality. I just kept searching, working, traveling, and seeking and along the way, I've discovered so many wonderful truths about who I am. My journey showed me what and who truly matters.

Every day, I continue to discover more about my life that IS out of the ordinary. Simply because, for better or worse, I have always followed my gypsy spirit. Following my inner voice hasn't always been easy. It takes courage, heart, power, resiliency, integrity, motivation, and a dash of crazy. However, I can say with 100% conviction that I would not have done it any other way, and I will always continue to follow my gypsy spirit. To know a gypsy is to love her because held within her is a pure love unlike any you have ever known. I believe you can feel this way as well, and maybe you already do.

The longer you live, the more similarities and contradictions you witness. The more you experience, the more compassionate or callused you can become. The gift is that you get to choose. How do *you* choose to perceive each experience in your life? Is it through a lens dictated by trauma from your experiences? If you expand your awareness about your past, you can understand that nothing in life has meaning except the meaning you give it. You alone must determine what an extraordinary life looks like for you *and* claim responsibility for taking the steps forward towards attaining it.

It's time to step up to your dreams and accept the life you crave!

Action Exercise:

- Paint me a picture using words or pictures, (whichever you prefer) detailing what *your* ideal life looks like.

_____

_____

_____

_____

_____

_____

_____

_____

_____

_____

_____

_____

_____

_____

_____

_____

_____

_____

_____

_____

_____

_____

_____

_____

_____

_____

You have been offered a set of tools that you can use to begin to create your most beautiful life. I hope that along the way you will continue to add additional tools to your tool belt that work for you. Think of your "tools" simply as a trait, talent, or experience that can help in your life. Whether they appear as knowledge or a new awareness through books, people or experiences, everything has an influence on you so choose how you spend your time wisely. One who fully embraces the road less traveled takes responsibility for searching out the best tools to use for creating their own happiness.

Right now, you are faced with the choice to own your power or not. I hope you choose to own it because you are worth it. From this day forward, opt for a new attitude, devoid of any thoughts of being a victim in any way. You are powerful, full of good and light, and you have just as much right as anyone else to achieve anything in life that you want. You are not better than anyone, nor are you below anyone else. I hope that you have begun to see yourself, as you truly are—a gypsy spirit who is ready to create! All that you have to do is claim it!

From here on out, choose to lead with your heart by making decisions based on your gut instinct. When you do, you will know that you are aligned with your gypsy spirit. Commit to sewing your awareness, intent, and highest good together. When they all flow together, watch out!

Caution: Anytime there is a lack of flow in your life and you become hell bent on "making things happen" or "figuring it all out," you lose. This happens when you are out of alignment with your gypsy spirit. In short, you are without a heartfelt intent so your actions are not in alignment with your heart or the flow of life.

Before I close this chapter, I want to help you understand the "flow of life" and the meaning behind it, as seen through a gypsy's eyes. Life is a river and you have four options:

1. Float down the river in a leisurely fashion allowing whatever comes your way to move you.
2. Hold on for dear life, refusing to make any choices, while white knuckling the side embankment and resisting any movement.
3. Swim against the current, hell bent on going in your own direction.
4. Enjoy the ride, feel the flow, and swim while glancing up every so often to make a choice as to which river you want to go with.

You may think gypsies only follow number #4 because it seems like the best choice for freedom and adventure. If that is what you thought you are right, it is the *best* scenario. However, the flow of life looks different at different times for each of us. Realize that you have a choice in every moment as to whether you will go with the flow or not. This includes deciding whether to lead with your head or your heart, or ideally creating a blend that works for you. Awareness is key on this journey so stay curious and in tune with your spirit, utilizing everything available to you.

Remember, no matter what we choose, there are valuable lessons for us. In moments of great resistance to life, I have learned important lessons that have offered me a much-needed deeper understanding. Whether white knuckling to hold onto to the bank of the river or struggling upstream against the current, there is great wisdom imparted following these actions. If nothing else, they allow greater wonderment when we finally put our head into the river and marvel at the flow of life like never before. This contrast offers us the ability to feel a great emergence of energy, power, allowance, and peace.

Your unique life is blossoming as you begin to understand that each moment in your past is an opportunity for understanding. Everything unfolded as it should in order to bring you right here, right now, ready to begin living your most sensational life. You are the most essential part of realizing your own happiness. Decide now that you *have* an amazing life, and commit from this day forward to making every day the most extraordinary adventure ever!

Action Exercise:

- What are you committed to in life?

  _____

  _____

  _____

  _____

  _____

- What are you willing to do to make your life beyond ordinary?

  _____

  _____

  _____

  _____

  _____

- In what ways can you make today more full of life, love, and connection?

  _____

  _____

  _____

  _____

  _____

- What daily actions can you take to make your days, weeks, and months your very own daring adventure?

  _____

  _____

  _____

  _____

  _____

DOODLE PAGE

XXI

come and gather

*"We imagine that we want to escape our
selfish and commonplace existence, but
we cling desperately to our chains."*

—ANNE SULLIVAN

Although we are nearing the end of this book, this is just
the beginning of your wonderful journey. Think of it like the
first day of the rest of your life! Before we go, I want you to
gather around so I can talk to you for a few more minutes
gypsies. That's right, come in close, let your bare feet soak
up the dark soft soil and sit on the stumps or directly on
the earth.

Let your body relax and breathe, letting go of any tension.
Let your head sway in front of you from side-to-side as you
breathe in the cleansing atmosphere. Now, open your eyes
if they are closed. Welcome. Today I am going to tell you a
story, one that you may have heard, but the take-away here
will be much different.

Like myself, you've probably heard a lot about Helen Keller, but far less about her guide, Anne Sullivan. Today, you are going to get to know more about her. Anne Sullivan lived a hard and love-deprived childhood. No stranger to death and scarcity, Anne's mother and most of her siblings died when she was young leaving her and one brother alone with an abusive father.

At five years old, Anne was sent to live with extended family where she contracted trachoma, a bacterial eye infection that left her half blind. Later, Anne and her brother were sent to a poorhouse where many mentally ill patients lived.

Shortly after, her brother passed away and once again, Anne was left entirely alone scarred by death, abuse, and very little love. Many have written about her "spunk" and strong will. I believe Anne had a strong gypsy spirit that was driven by adversity to learn and succeed for a greater purpose.

The story continues...one day in 1880, the head of the state school board visited Tewksbury for an inspection. Anne had heard about this school and apparently intended to go there. She told the visitor this and somehow her wish was granted. Not long after, she began attending Perkins Institution for the Blind in Boston, Massachusetts.

Even though Anne did not fit in with her peers for most of her childhood, there was something undeniably special about her. When she was 20 years old, Anne was named the valedictorian at graduation where she delivered an unforgettable speech.

It is inspiring to me that Anne raised herself, making her own way in the world. She learned at a young age that if she wanted to do something and make something of herself, it was up to her to. Those steps were not easy but she dug deep and triumphed. Of this she speaks:

"People seldom see the halting and painful steps by which the most insignificant success is achieved."

-ANNE SULLIVAN

I know you are going to have to dig deep and that some of the steps you take will be filled with darkness. Yet, I want you to know that you can do it, just like Anne did. No one saw Anne overcome the trials and hardships in her early childhood and maybe no one will ever see you overcome yours. Those dark places are significant but no more than the work you are doing right now with me. No matter who you are or where you have been, you can *choose* the direction of your life. You can break free from any chains that are holding you back, preventing you from realizing your own freedom. This reminds me of a wonderful quote by Esther Hicks-

"If you knew your potential to feel good, you would ask no one to be different so that you can feel good. You would free yourself of all of that cumbersome impossibility of needing to control the world, or control your mate, or control your child. You are the only one who creates your reality. For no one else can think for you, no one else can do it. It is only you, every bit of it you."

- ESTHER HICKS

Of course, Anne became Helen Keller's guide, teacher, mentor, and friend and we know the miraculous story of Anne teaching Helen. Did you also know they continued to live together for their entire lives as lifelong friends?

It is known that Helen needed Anne. It is lesser known that Anne needed Helen. I believe we all need companionship, mentoring, and someone to give us meaning. Does this feel true to you? Is life not a dance—a give and take? We see balance at every turn, like the yin and yang of our lives. When I look at Helen Keller, I see Anne Sullivan. Without Anne, Helen quite possibly would have failed to "see" life in the beautiful manner that Anne taught her.

Likewise, Helen became Anne's focus. She was able to use all of her experiences, pouring them into one human being who needed her. Helen gave Anne's life meaning by helping her to realize her purpose, utilizing her skills and talents.

We all need a guide—an Anne Sullivan to push us to realize our dreams. Most of us have many people who love, support, and encourage us, but they aren't the best ones to direct us because typically, they love us regardless of any outcomes, as it ought to be. As much as we love them and them us, dear gypsies, in order to be truly successful in achieving what we want to, we need a mentor like Anne.

Imagine a group of like-minded gypsies around you who ensure you live your most daring adventure by making sure you remain accountable to what you say you will do. In fact, accountability is the one thing that holds most people back from what they truly want in life.

I am the guide that unites you together with other passionately purposeful, free-spirited gypsies so together we can contribute to a cause that is much larger than we are. What if one gypsy community could make all that difference for you? I believe in this because I experienced the huge difference one person made in my life. It is my belief that part of my calling is to bring us together in community so that you have the opportunity to find the person you have been searching for.

I believe the Gypsy Living Community will unite women on this planet to create a healing power like never before. Together, we can create a community that is not lead by one, but linked by like-minded gypsies who want to serve, and in turn be served. If you were unsure of your mission in life and you feel something stirring in you now, allow me to be the first to welcome you to your life mission, where you will give, serve, and receive more than you ever thought possible.

I am passionate about creating an entire network of gypsies that physically and virtually connect, heal, plan, and prepare for the most amazing future ever.

Remember, it was said by the brilliant Albert Einstein,

> "THE MORE *I* LEARN, THE MORE *I* REALIZE HOW MUCH *I* DON'T KNOW."

Keep learning my gypsies and never stop stretching and growing. Whether it is with me, my books, community, and other gypsy resources, or the myriad of other exceptional teachers out there. Keep your curiosity alive. It is that hunger for understanding, truth, and connection that has brought me to you.

I want to thank you for being a part of my journey. As I look at each one of you, I see life, laughter, and enjoyment. I see confidence, power, humility, and grace. When I look at you, I see the real you, as I hope you look at me, and see the real me.

It is my honor to welcome you to the gypsy life. You have now unleashed your inner gypsy and are ready to live an adventurous life, each day for the rest of your life! As we gather in a group hug, accepting of the paths we have all traveled, we come together with a force that is more powerful than swords or guns. United in a cause that is true, open, and clear. The light in me, honoring the light in you shines, and together we create a glow that lights the forest we are in. Ever so slowly, as you gaze down on the dark forest floor, you see a light. It may be small and singular at first, however, over the next days, weeks, months, and years, that light will become so bright it will cover the world.

This powerful healing light will cover you and the entire Earth. As it surrounds and encompass the wounded who feel alone, it will heal the broken hearts, surpass the wrongful deaths, and embrace the good, the light, and truth in each of us. It connects you to me, and us to those across the universe in this mysterious wonder we call life. Together we are united in a cause that can only come together when each of us is living fully in our consciousness of our own gypsy spirit where we are aligned with our own personal power.

As we become whom we are meant to, by letting go of the ego, images, and relationships, we create the space to become who we will, can, and must become. **Your journey awaits.**

As we near the end of our book journey this poem exemplifies the bridge we have traveled on.

"The bridge will only take you halfway there, to those mysterious lands you long to see. Through gypsy camps and swirling Arab fair, and moonlit woods where unicorns run free. So come and walk awhile with me and share the twisting trails and wondrous worlds I've known. But this bridge will only take you halfway there. The last few steps you have to take alone."

—SHEL SILVERSTEIN

There is so much more knowledge and information for you to dedicate your time and energy to. If you do, I promise you will live your most daring adventure. I know if you implement these gypsy ways, no matter your pace, they will allow you the time and space to change your life. I know this because living this way has changed mine. It may not always be easy to accomplish what we want in life, but it is possible.

"It does not matter how slowly you go as long as you do not stop."

-CONFUCIUS

You are possible. You are capable. You are enough. You are worthy and you are now a gypsy! YES, YOU!

Embrace and own who you are and your inherent qualities that make you YOU! Be happy, smile at yourself and others, and show the world you are not afraid to be you. Each day be grateful for your gypsy spirit and that you are not like anyone else.

With much love, I release you to your journey and welcome you into the Gypsy Living Community. You are mine and I am yours, and together we will create the future.

The world needs more gypsies; the world needs more of you. Be bold, break out, and unleash your very own gypsy spirit.

> *"Do not go where the path may lead, go instead where there is no path and leave a trail."*

-RALPH WALDO EMERSON

You and only you, hold the key.

XO
Andrea

DOODLE PAGE

about the author

Andrea Blosch Riggs is the author who articulated the essence of the *Gypsy Living* mindset through her own life experiences fueled by her unquenchable curiosity.

It was during her family's move from Southern Utah to Puerto Rico that the inspiration for *Gypsy Living* was born. After they returned to Southern Utah to build their dream home and raise chickens, goats, and sheep, Andrea documented this change in pace on her podcast, *Gypsy Fam* on iTunes.

Andrea loves mothering three mini gypsies, and being a wife to a thrill-seeking skydiver, computer geek, and gut healer. You can usually find her practicing yoga, teaching at a conference, writing, making fermented foods or baking her infamous brownies, kissing and playing with her kids, at the beach or adventuring, or teaching others so do the same.

If you are interested in Andrea's talents as an author, speaker, presenter, movement leader, yoga teacher, gut-health and energy healer, you can learn more about her and her passions at www.gypsyfam.com.

Two favors for me:

1. Rate *Gypsy Living* on Amazon with your honest feedback. This is more helpful to the growth of this movement than you realize. Thank you so much!

2. Connect with me on social media and take a picture of you with the book and use #LiveGypsy. Any adventure or life event that reminds you of unleashing your gypsy spirit tag, share, and show the world just how magical you really are. #LiveGypsy

3. Find out how Andrea's Guide program can help you live your most daring adventure everyday by going to www.gypsyfam.com and Click on GUIDE PROGRAM.

CONNECT TO THE MOTHER GYPSY

If you like what you have read or listened to, subscribe to my website www.gypsyfam.com and connect with me on social media to hear about the launch of my upcoming magical trifecta books.

10% of all GypsyFam profits go to the Africa Yoga Project. To find out more go to https://www.africayogaproject.org

acknowledgments

A very special thank you to my children—Lucy, Evan and Ava—for being patient with me through this journey and allowing me to implement the term 'gypsy spirit' into our daily vocabulary.

I know it's not always as cool as one may think to have someone like me as their mother. I love each of you more than you can comprehend. Thank you for inspiring me on a daily basis to live my most daring adventure.

To the Universe—thank you for sending me thousands of guides along my path to help me during my own journey of unleashing my gypsy spirit.

To my editor Amy—thank you for making my words come to life better than I ever could, and to Julie for introducing us.

To Ashely and Lindsay—thank you for helping me find my branding gypsy, Tuesday. To my mastermind gypsies—Bree, Nat and Linds—I adore you.

To my amazing Dad, Mom, and sisters—Lisa, Amy and Angie—for being on this journey with me. I love you all so much.

To all of my family, friends, and mentors in life—thank you for supporting me. Bountiful Utah childhood friends—thank you for always making me feel fourteen again.

Thank you to all of you who've impacted my career and strengthened my resolve to dream bigger and work harder. I am grateful for those in work, play, conferences, and fitness who have sweated and shook it with me for over a decade. For those who have blessed my life in fitness, nutrition and fermentation, and connection. For my fellow yoga lovers, especially the Baptiste Yoga Community, who have changed the course of my life for the better. For my clients and students who've continually blessed my life and expanded my heart. The depth of my knowledge stems from beautiful souls who have touched my soul and have shared a piece of their heart with me. I am forever grateful.

Lastly to the love of my life Charles—the biggest thank you for always loving and believing in me. Especially for the gentle nudge to write what I know to be true and helping me refine my message again and again. May you always be in my sight and grasp. I love you baby!

57859830R00180

Made in the USA
San Bernardino, CA
23 November 2017